CATCH THE WIND

FATHER
JOHN O'BRIEN OFM

CATCH THE WIND

FATHER
JOHN O'BRIEN OFM

Pen Press
London

First Published in Great Britain in 1996 by
Pen Press
Church House
Portland Avenue
Stamford Hill
London N16 6HJ

ISBN 1 900796 10 4

A catalogue record of this book is available
from the British Library.

Front cover - Starry Night by Vincent Van Gogh
Courtesy of Museum of Modern Art, New York

Printed by Hobbs the Printers Ltd, Totton, Hampshire

To Robina Burke

Aknowledgements:

Many thanks to Assumpta Galvin
who typed my manuscript,
and to
Richard Graham, Roscrea, Co Tipperary,
who typeset the work.

J. O'B., Athlone, 1996

Typography and composition:
RICHARD GRAHAM
CEDAR HILL, ROSCREA, CO. TIPPERARY

Contents

An Introduction

"In the chilly hours and minutes of uncertainty
I want to be in the warm heart of your love and
mine,
to feel you all around me and to take your hand,
along the sand,
"Ah, but I may as well try to catch the wind."

THIS is the opening of a Donovan song. It's lonely and has always struck a chord with me. Later on in the song he speaks of rain 'hanging on the leaves like tears'. The mood caught for me is one of emerging loneliness. The 'chilly hours and moments of uncertainty' is something that comes to all at one moment or another. It can come in the form of changes in the state of life, in illness, in confused questions about what was once held dear but now a whole world has changed. It can come in personal trauma, abuse by a loved and trusted one, in having to face a sudden and debilitating illness. When one is in such a world, the heart becomes something of a lonely hunter. We search for comfort, for love, for something, or someone, to ease the heartache. We are too broken, however, to find peace or to trust love, and our brokenness can be a wound unhealed. The motif 'Catch the Wind' is a metaphor for our confused search for love and belonging. So often our search appears useless and leading to mere loneliness; still, it is my metaphor for 'longing loneliness'.

I have had my own battle to fight against longing loneliness:

not always successful – everything appeared like 'Chasing the Wind', but I do know that at different times I have discovered people who shared after my troubled world, and gave me hope sometimes to 'hope against hope'.

It was in this search that I re-discovered the Bible and, more particularly, the biblical authors, their storytelling and their narrative style. I remember an interview with Stephen King given on the *Book Show* on Sky News. He spoke of story and storytelling in general – then in relation to his own works.

He spoke of his fears, worries and love. His stories began here, and he worked out his fears in storytelling. "Stories save lives," he said.

The interview helped me to appreciate the Bible more, and allowed me to appreciate the way the biblical authors communicated. Some books embrace poetry, which involves the reader and helps gain for him a new perspective on reality. Other books are true stories, but the truth is filtered to us through a human agency and involves his art of storytelling. Other books involve reflections on life and the authors' views on life. In these the authors tell their own stories – if indirectly – and involve us. All the books, in their different forms, involve us, and lead us to see the world from a different perspective. Sometimes we can be led to see God and ourselves in a different light, and come to a different consciousness of ourselves and God, and so change our relationship. This is the world where I best try to come to terms with my longing loneliness, where I try to 'Catch the Wind'. The following lines occur as a prelude to what hopefully will be more detailed meditations on Scripture, suffering, loneliness and life.

A live dog is better than a dead lion. (Ecc 9:14)

The first Author I fell in love with was Qoheleth (Ecclesiastes). When I first began studying the Bible, I wondered what Qoheleth would have to say. If it was in the matter of giving comfort, then I found that Qoheleth was, well, different. I found such 'joyful' pieces as: 'Sheer futility,' Qoheleth says, 'sheer futility; everything is futile.' (Ecc 1:2)

It was not what I expected, but I loved it instantly. Qoheleth did not have a good relationship with God, had difficulty knowing and finding his place in the scheme of things. All of this comes out in a negative, pessimistic man of the world. He appears as one who is hurt. He describes all as vanity and 'Chasing the Wind'. He is important in his pessimistic viewpoint because he puts words on the feelings of searching in vain and loneliness. Indeed his despondency involves me in his world, but this helps me always to come to terms with my loneliness, even though this can be 'Vanity and Chasing the Wind', or at times appear to be so.

Exile on Main Street

The next book that gives me hope in my life's battles is *Job*.

I had the picture in my head from 'common wisdom' that Job was patient, and was something of a 'goody-goody' – he was, but this was not the whole story.

James, in his letter, speaks of the perseverance of Job as a model for us. It is strange what opening and reading the *Book of Job* did for me. *Job* is a drama, with Job and the three comforters who, in their blindness, try to convince Job that his sufferings are there for a good reason.

They break Job's heart but he counters, challenging their assumptions, their wisdom and ultimately the God they claim to represent. Job finds himself angry and totally alone – he is the architypical 'Exile on Main Street'. The man feels he has lost God.

The drama is powerful. Illness and trauma can lead one to feel as if one were all – alone, that God no longer loves one or that, if He did, feel He no longer cares, and I was not patient with my pain or grief. *Job* gives me a perspective on my behalf, and the relief that comes at the end of the Book, as the relationship between Job and God is restored, is welcome. For Job says our pain, our wounded feelings, do belong in the eyes of God. When I was crushed and done for, I did not really believe this – Job bade me think again.

Love is Strong as Death

The *Song of Songs* is not a story in any sense. It is a collection of love poems. In them, however, is described the topsy-turvy world of relationships. Relationships are a mine-strewn area, and it is so easy to get hurt and be lonelier still.

The poems describe moments of intimacy, of loss, of shame, of misunderstanding and of starting all-over again. Yet this is presented in rich poetry and one knows this is a good world to be in after all, because 'Love is strong as Death'.

The theme of human love is what is central in the *Song of Songs*, but it does open the way for us to appreciate the Divine. The one thing that can heal our loneliness is the power of love.

If you see Him say hello

This chapter began by accident. I was working on Mark – John Mark in *Acts* – and noticed his cousin disappeared. Then I discovered that Paul and Barnabas had a fight over John Mark and parted violently. I am sure that text was always there but I have never really given it the attention it deserved.

It was important for Mark because he was later reconciled to Paul, and in his Gospel the theme of reconciliation is crucial. I could not but feel sorry for the great-hearted Barnabas, who did so much for Paul and now found himself dismissed.

In the last few years, I had come to see the humanness of the biblical authors, and I came to see in the story 'good people do disagree', and here we find the work of God; Paul's letters and Mark's Gospel grow from these people and situations. Sometimes relationships suffer for a while due to our hard-heartedness. This is the down-side of the *Song of Songs* in that love can be lost for a while, but we have to begin again.

Mark's Passion

On the cross Jesus spoke only a few words, but his act of accepting death is God's word saying, 'I love you'. This is mediated to us through human authors, and I chose Mark because of the starkness of his account. This account is all the more richer because of his – Mark's – experience of running away from Paul, and finding himself unforgiven until much later in life. He also stood beside Peter in his last days and showed his true mettle in Rome. The theme of discipleship is central in Mark, and he shows in the story of Peter that one might not always get things right.

It is to the Cross that we bring our woundedness, and this enables us to hear Jesus saying, 'I love you,' and helps us remember that 'Love is strong as Death'.

Epilogue: Letter to Philemon

I finish with Paul in all this letter. Philemon has a runaway slave, Onesimus, and now he has to face a new situation as a Christian in a Christian household.

When we are suffocated by loneliness and the sense of longing, when everything in the world seems to conspire and thwart us, then we are in the same boat – we have to find answers to the new questions, and we have to try and listen for God's help. This can appear like vanity and chasing of the wind, but there is always something in us that will try and catch the wind and lead life to the full.

It's hard to sum up, in just a few words, what my meditations are all about. What I bring to what I read is my own experiences. The different events I chose in my meditations helped give me a perspective on my own troubles and hopes. By involving me in various and different ways I find I am not alone.

I remember one of the lines from the film *Shadowlands.* One of C.S. Lewis's students said to him: "We read to know we are not alone."

I hope not just that I am not alone, but that I will find the peace that God alone can give. Somehow I know all is not vanity and chasing the wind!

I share these meditations with you, because I hope you can find yourself in the stories and come to find your peace.

Chapter One

A living dog is better than a dead lion.

THE Author of the *Book of Ecclesiastes* finds himself in a world that, in his perception, has become hostile and threatening. In trying to relate to the world, Ecclesiastes, or Qoholeth, finds himself oppressed and pessimistic in the face of vanity, as he sees it.

"I, Qololeth, have reigned in Jerusalem over Isræl.
With the help of wisdom I have been at pains to
study all that is done under heaven; oh, what a
weary task God has given mankind to labour at! I
have seen everything that is done under the sun, and
what vanity it all is, what chasing of the wind!
What is not there cannot be straightened,
what is not there cannot be counted.
I thought to myself, 'I have acquired a greater stock
of wisdom than any of my predecessors in Jerusalem.
I have great experience of wisdom and learning.'
Wisdom has been my careful study: stupidity, too,
and folly. And now I have come to recognise that
even this is chasing of the wind.
Much wisdom, much grief,
the more knowledge, the more sorrow." (Ecc. 1:12–18)

The Author here appears to identify himself with Solomon, but it is now thought he came from the post-exilic period. His assertion comes from the language used and the sense of pessimism that pervaded that period.

Qoholeth has come to fascinate me, and in many ways has purified my faith. At one stage I had a more naïve view of what

7

belonged to the Bible. Then I came across Qoholeth and his world-weary view, I could not immediately see how he belonged. Then I learned that it was in the IVth Century AD that he was finally accepted.

I could see that there were many others who felt something like I did. Qoholeth performed a critical assessment of theology, of conventional wisdom and piety. This constitutes an attempt, not to denigrate these, but an attempt to keep religion honest and in touch with reality. Reality is the touchstone used by Qoholeth to test the tenets of common wisdom. The book also insists on enjoyment, and there is an important voice to be heard by anyone who locates the measure of biblical religion more in asceticism than in love and social concern, and who feel that biblical religion in some ways militates against enjoyment.

Qoholeth, too, has a negative assessment of the workaholic. This is a neat counterbalance for those who posit the belief that workaholism has a value of itself, or is synonymous with religious dedication. Here again, Qoholeth goes against the common wisdom of his time, of the time of the Industrial Revolution, and indeed of today, when not a few people see workaholism as some kind of virtue, and are quick to call in the deity to reinforce their not-quite-threatened position. I know that I have often been subjected to 'common wisdom' statements of my time, such as: 'The devil makes work for idle hands.' 'Hard work never killed anyone,' and 'Nobody ever died of hard work.' As we saw in Ecc. 1:16–18 Qoholeth was not buying into this world-view, and even—especially—today, his more human touch is vitally needed.

I know myself that I have been left with the impression that I, and all the Faithful, should be experiencing a relationship of a close personal kind with God. When God has seemed far away, and life totally confusing, when loneliness and a sense of failure and worthlessness were dark and uninvited guests in my house, then I felt a profound sense of loss and dis-ease. Qoholeth felt something like this. Many people have to travel in the dark night of faith, as Qoholeth did, and what the book of Qoholeth does is allow those, who search in the dark, their dignity in the believing community, because Qoholeth himself was deemed worthy to have a place among the biblical writings. Yes, indeed, there is a need for Qoholeth to be supplemented by other biblical books, but this voice too deserves to be heard.

The Thought of Qoholeth

For starter, Qoholeth does believe in God and in the fear of God.

> "I know that what God does HE does consistently. To this nothing can be added, for this nothing is taken away, yet God sees to it that men fear Him." (3:14)

He too believes in an ethical code and in God's judgement on human behaviour.

> "Rejoice in your youth, you who are young;
> let your heart give you joy in your young days.
> Follow the prompting of your heart
> and the desires of your eyes.
> But this you must know: for all these things God will
> bring you to judgement.
> Cast worry from your heart,
> shield your flesh from pain.
> Yet youth, the age of dark hair, is vanity." (11:9, 12:1)

Here we see that Qoholeth's relationship with God is not of a warm personal nature. Indeed his view of God must be further tinted by the fact that he does not believe in an afterlife.

> "Whatever work you propose to do, do it while you can,
> for there is neither achievement, nor planning, nor
> knowledge, nor wisdom in Sheol where you are going."
> (9:10)

Sheol is an abode for the dead, and is not equal to our life everlasting with God. Qoholeth shows the pain of distance between himself and an intimate relationship with God. The world then appears to him as a dark place, a world of vanity and 'chasing the wind'.

"All things are wearisome." (1:8)

Although Qoholeth finds things difficult, he does not recommend a foolish abandoning of wisdom, of faith, and an embracing of any opposing views. While things are 'wearisome' he does not promote despair. He believes, with the wise men of his age, that God has given everything its appropriate time.

"A time for giving birth;
a time for dying;
a time for planting;
a time for uprooting what has been planted.
    "A time for killing;
a time for healing;
a time for knocking down;
a time for building.
    "A time for tears;
a time for laughter;
a time for mourning;
a time for dancing.
    "A time for throwing stones away,
a time for gathering them up;
a time for embracing.
    "A time for searching,
a time for losing;
a time for keeping,
a time for throwing away.
    "A time for tearing,
a time for sewing;
a time for keeping silent,

a time for speaking.
"A time for loving,
a time for hating;
a time for way,
a time for peace." (3:1–11)

God has also given to humanity the ability of enjoyment.

"There is no happiness for man but to eat and drink and be content with his work. This, too, I see as something from God's hand, since plenty and penury both come from God; wisdom, knowledge, joy, He gives to the man who pleases Him; on the sinner He lays the task of gathering and storing up for another who is pleasing to God. This, to, is vanity and chasing of the wind." (2:24–36)

The word 'vanity' is a favourite word of Qoholeth. He uses it thirty-seven times in the book. It comes from the Hebrew word 'hebel'. The Hebrew word means, literally, breath or vapour, and designates what is transient and lacking in substance. Qoholeth is arguing that, whatever happens, it has long since been 'named', and the man is:

"unable to argue with one that is stronger than he." (6:10)

It is as if one has been predetermined, and not to accept one's fate, one's time, is to disavow any chance of happiness. God has 'made' not only the days of prosperity, but the days of adversity, and thus they have to be endured.

For Qoholeth, the knowledge he has about God, and the control He has over the world, does not give ease to his troubled mind: quite the opposite in fact. What happens for the one who sets out to master life? This is Qoholeth's answer:

"What does a man gain for the efforts he makes? I contemplate the tasks that God gives mankind to labour at. All that He does is apt for its time; but, though He

has permitted men to consider time in its wholeness,
man cannot comprehend the work of God from
beginning to end." (3:9–11)

For Qoholeth, his trouble lies in the fact that man cannot
find out what God has done! Man is unable to see what has
been decreed by God. This is what he means when he says that
man does not know his time. Blind and unsuspecting, like
animals blundering in a net, he is suddenly overtaken by evil
time. (9:12) It is also God who made the evil day, but this
ultimately is of no consolation, for man is unable to discover
what comes after him. (7:14)

"But there is vanity found on earth; the good, I mean,
receive the treatment the wicked deserve; and the
wicked the treatment the good deserve. This, too, I say,
is vanity." (8:14–15)

Traditional theology had said that the good would prosper
and the wicked would not (8:12–14), but here we see that the
test of reality and experience shows this to be false. These
events set up an insurmountable barrier, which is set against his
search for knowledge.

We have here a picture of a lonely Qoholeth. Things do not
make sense; what he had believed once is sadly no more, and
Qoholeth feels all alone in his world, where things are not
squaring up, where everything is now vanity. He believes in
God, but what he learned earlier about God, and the reward for
the just and the punishment of the wicked does not match
reality. He has come to know God all over again.

Is there any value in life at all for Qoholeth? Since God has
made the good day and the bad day (7:14), man can still hold
himself ready, with a completely open mind for whatever God
is ready to grant him:

"In the day of prosperity be joyful." (7:14)

Here for Qoholeth is the point in which God deals with man. The question of man's lot—i.e. of the place assigned to him, in modern parlance a question of meaning—is where one can recognise a divine intention directed for the person's good. This is the only thing one can call 'good', that a man should enjoy his work, for this is his lot (3:22, 5:17). Here Qoholeth sees he is in accord with a divine purpose—here he sees himself closest to God:

"... for there is nothing better for a man than he should eat and drink and enjoy himself. I see that too comes from God's hand." (2:24)

He speaks excitedly on the subject again:

"Go, eat your bread with joy
and drink your wine with a glad heart;
for what you do God has approved beforehand.
Wear white all the time,
do not stint your head of oil.
Spend your time with the woman you love, through all
the fleeting days of the life that God has given you
under the sun; for this is the lot assigned to you in life
and in the efforts you exert under the sun. Whatever
work you propose to do, do it while you can, for there
is neither achievement, nor planning, nor knowledge,
nor wisdom in Sheol where you are going." (9:7–10)

Qoholeth is not presenting us with any self-contained compendium of instructions. He brings the reader into play. Confronted by Qoholeth's sense of melancholy, one realises that one has found a kindred spirit, who struggles to make sense of the world. He facilitates the searcher in making a breakthrough from the dogmatic, well-ordered world to a more realistic and truer view of the world.

Qoholeth confronts the wisdom of his time with his own and others' experience. His once safe world has disintegrated, and he finds himself in a lonely place.

This journey is made over and over again by different people, in different times and different places. For example, many Catholics who lived with a different idea of morality, faith and liturgical worship, find themselves in grief over a world they were asked to let go of, and find themselves in a lonely place wondering just what is right. Anybody who has tried to live up to an ideal, and then found they culled no longer hold on to that world they once believed in, find themselves in that lonely place too. Those who have tried to find God and follow Him in their lives, can, at times, live through lonely nights where nothing seems to be right. This, too, is a melancholic lonely place. Although permeated by God, the world becomes silent.

"That which happens is far off, deep, very deep. Who can find it out." (7:14)

"Even in his own loving and hating, man is unable to understand himself." (9:1)

Man can never achieve a dialogue with his surroundings, still less with God. Is God still, then, a 'Thou'? Even if God grants fulfilment in life, this is no more than a gift handed silently over. Qoholeth has set out to answer the question of the meaning of life, the question about man's lot, without having any confidence himself in life.

Further Aspect of Qoholeth's Thought

Qoholeth's quarrel is with any thought that ignores experience and tends to become unreal. Thus he attacks the simplistic statements of the traditional idea of retribution:

"But I still observe that under the sun crime is where the law should be, the criminal where the good should be. 'God,' I thought to myself, 'will judge both virtuous and criminal, because there is a time here for all that is purposed or done.' I also thought that mankind behaves like this so that God may show them up for the brute beasts they are to each other. Indeed the fate of man and beast is identical; one dies, the other too, and both have the self-same breath; man has no advantage over the beast, for all is vanity." (3:16–19)

Qoholeth sees death as the leveller, and indeed for him the end of life. 'Sheol' was the abode of the dead, and welcomed man and beast, good and bad, into oblivion. Qoholeth could now see, as he arrived at the statement, that things were not as they should be. He is not optimistic about the human quest for wisdom.

"I, Qoholeth, have reigned in Jerusalem over Israel. With the help of wisdom I have been at pains to study all that is done under heaven; oh, what a weary task God has given mankind to labour at! I have seen everything that is done under the sun, and what vanity it all is, what chasing of the wind!

"What is twisted cannot be straightened,
what is not there cannot be counted.

"I thought to myself, 'I have acquired a greater stock of wisdom than any of my predecessors in Jerusalem. I have greater experience of wisdom and learning.' Wisdom has been my careful study; stupidity, too, and folly. And now I have come to recognise that even this is chasing of the wind. Much wisdom, much grief the more knowledge, the more sorrow." (1:12–18)

Qoholeth might not feel at home in our world today. There are many examples of groups talking of self-actualisation and self-realisation. Qoholeth's pessimism might not be a theme in the face of this optimism. Perhaps both are needed to challenge and enrich each other. Crass pessimism can destroy, but naive optimism about people and events, is infinitely more destructive, as the expectation values can be set too high.

Qoholeth also challenges the traditional—in his time!—emphasis on industriousness, if it means total absorption in work, because such feverish labour robs one of enjoyment.

> "... for what does a man gain for all the toll and strain that he has undergone under the sun? What of all his laborious days, his cares of office, his restless nights? This, too, is vanity." (2:22–23)

I have often wondered was Qoholeth autobiographical in these words. He does not say so, but the strength of feeling here would suggest he had intimate contact with what he was speaking about. He sounds like someone burnt-out and stressed-out.

I find the age we live in to be similar to Qoholeth's; to be more exact, I find the spirit of Qoholeth's age to be alive today in quite a number of people. They spend hours working, and then boast of how hard work is—I am not impressed, but I try not to let on. I found a statement of Norman Vincent Peale helpful here: I remember him saying that he believed in working hard, but not hard work. The industriousness and slavish devotion to work can slowly strangle life. Qoholeth is here arguing strongly to do one's work, but not to be suffocated by over-work or burnt-out; this is the inner meaning of one's time.

Not all Qoholeth's observations are easy to take. He is very definitely anti-woman:

> "Once again I was at pains to study wisdom and retribution, to see wickedness as folly, and foolishness as madness. I find woman more bitter than death; she is a snare, her heart a net, her arms are chains; he who is pleasing to God eludes her, but the sinner is her captive. This you must know, says Qoholeth, is the sum of my investigation, putting this and that together.

I have made other researches too, without result.
"One man in a thousand I may find,
but never a woman better than the rest." (7:25–29)

If one looks closely at Qoholeth's findings, one can see that his anti-woman stance is not exactly pro-man. He might find a good man in a thousand—not good odds. It is at this point I feel my saddest for Qoholeth; he comes across as a broken, confused, bitter human being, who can find no solace, and he pushes people away from him because his loneliness is almost complete.

Seeing the world through the eyes f loneliness can present distorted pictures of people. Indeed, not 'can' but 'does'. His words are harsh but they are born of deep anguish. Nailed to the cross of loneliness, one should not expect moving speeches about people and relationships. Cruel words expose a cruel loneliness that is in the heart of Qoholeth, our lonely seeker.

Qoholeth in the Progress of Revelation

The reflections of Qoholeth are centred on the nothingness of earthly pleasures. He, as it were, by being true to his own truth, co-operates with the spirit of God in sowing the seeds of the development of the understanding of God, and the seeker before God. Insistence on the person's responsibility for his acts, permitted the notion of the importance of the individual to emerge. (Jer. 31:29–30; Ez. 18:33) The wise sages had to come to the realisation that the thought of temporal happiness as a good in itself, would have to be abandoned.

Centuries of accepted world-views were now being threatened, and this is hard to take on board. The beliefs that sustained people were now being challenged. Qoholeth would, in his own inimitable way, safeguard the dignity of those who found themselves in a melancholic, questioning place. Others would find their faith shattered by the experience of exile, and now their traditional wisdom was under challenge, and this challenge was the challenge of experience.

Neither world was a safe place to be in, and both sides would come to the inevitable questions:

'Is there anything we can cling to?'
'What can we believe?'
'Is there any hope left for us?'
'Where are You, God?'
'Do You care?'
'Do You hear?'
'Is there life after death?'

It is due to these holy people struggling with their faith that God was able to work. The ground was prepared for His revelation in Jesus Christ. Qoholeth affirms the vanity of earthly things, and thus prepares the mind of his disciples towards a 'beyond the grave' preceded by the judgement of God. (12:13) *The Book of Wisdom* (Ch, 2–5) has re-echoes of *Daniel* (12–13), the faith of the seven martyred brothers and their mother (2Mc 7,9), as well as the conviction of Judas Maccabeus (2Mc 12:43–46) will open horizons on the destiny of humankind which Christ will illumine (Mk 5:3–11, 25:31–46; Lk 16:19–31).

Qoholeth and Prayer

"How else but through a broken heart can Lord Christ enter in?" asked Oscar Wilde. When our world is in tatters and we feel crushed, then we are disposed to seek out words and people to heal us.

"Come to Me, all who are weary and are overburdened, and I will give you rest. Shoulder My Yoke and learn for Me for I am gentle and humble in heart, and you will find rest for your souls. Yes My Yoke is easy and My burden light." (Mtt 11:28–39)

Qoholeth in his depression, his sense of burn-out, speaks for those souls whose lives are troubled and nothing seems to fit. His perception of the world and of people, is clouded by the pain he feels inside. He has his own truth, his own heart, and he has seen so much disappointment in life that he is 'weary and overburdened'. To express this condition as starkly as Qoholeth comes as something of a shock—but not to Jesus. He responds to the pain of those who struggle and He comes to give us repose. Qoholeth did not see Jesus in his lifetime, but as we saw, by being firm in his truth, he did not abandon God, but ultimately prepared the way so that Jesus could come and give rest to the weary.

His words, written all those years before Jesus, bring to my mind some of John of the Cross's dark night. His dark night applies to Christian souls advancing in prayer, but part of his explanation is very applicable to Qoholeth.

> "... (the soul) suffers great pain and grief, since there is added to all this (because of the solitude and abandonment caused in it by the dark night) the fact it finds no consolation or support in anything."
>
> (Dark Night of the Soul XI,7)

The dark night is a stage of growth on the way to coming to know God. Night describes for John the spiritual desolation one goes through.

> "Oh night which guided me!
> Oh night more lovely than the dawn!
> Oh night which joined
> Beloved with lover,
> Love transformed in the Beloved!" (Dark Night V,5)

Love transforms, even for a while our world is darkness, for we are not alone.

> "I live in holy heights
> but I am with the contrite and humble,
> to revive the spirit of the humble,
> to revive the heart of the contrite." (Is 557:15)

Life is still meant to be lived

Our book approaches despair but does not get there, and that is important. To achieve greatness, acquire wealth and wisdom and become all that society advises is to chase after the wind. We can feel the wind. We know its presence but we can not see its beginning nor its end. It eludes our grasp or control and, in the ancient world, even escaped our understanding.

Qoholeth is exercising suspicion of his society's values. On one hand, Qoholeth claims that God and the Divine plan are unknowable, but, on the other hand, he claims himself to know something about God and the Divine plan. For instance, from the hand of God comes the gifts of eating, drinking and toil (2:24). In short, for Qoholeth life is a gift and we deserve a quality of life. This is, perhaps too, a key to understanding his pessimism. In life we find injustice (3:16–18), (4:1), human contradictions (3:11) and fruitless toil (8:16–17). These experiences are part and parcel of my own experience and baggage. Qoholeth brings the experiences and his reactions centre-stage. Feelings of despondency and hurt that arise in connection with life's sadness have to be acknowledged.

My language is very much the language of the Twentieth Century, and Qoholeth would not have thought in present-day categories, but he was brave enough to formulate his feelings in his own time, in his own way, and to start a dialogue across the centuries. Qoholeth came across a world that was sadder than he hoped for, or expected, and this brought him to the brink of despair, but not beyond. He expressed, in his work, his trouble with workaholism, injustice, not understanding God or others at times, and ultimately finding himself lonely (7:25–29). In a human being whre there are psychological wounds, these too need healing. If the wounds of the spirit are repressed, in time they become poisonous and lead ultimately to despair. Qoholeth comes forward in his word, and showed the things that were wounding his spirit; only when they could be healed can human beings live life to the full (c2:24, 3:12, 22; 5:18–19, 9:7,9).

This is why Qoholeth is such a strong character for me. He expresses openly and honestly how he sees things. In our repressed generation, such honesty is not always to be found. It is so true that for many people denial is the operative word. The Alcoholic denies that he or she has a problem. Those who abuse sexually are blind to the pain they inflict, not just the physical, but the emotional fallout that the abused carries until he/she admits that life is too hard ('absurd', 'vanity': 'chasing the wind'). Admitting to a problem, and that life has lost its flavour, is the first step to healing. It is not healing, but the healing process has been set in motion, and that is the beginning of new life.

I see Qoholeth as being brave enough in his time to set out how despondent one can be in the face of life, but time and time again he sets before the reader the chance of living life to the full. We can only adjust at the problems of life by admitting at this time that things can be bad, and we stand bruised and broken in the need of love. We are called to a better quality of life:

"Go eat your bread with enjoyment and drink your wine with a merry heart for God has always approved what you do. Let your garments always be white; let not oil be lacking on your head." (9:7)

Life can be lonely, but something makes us fight on to come to a better quality of life for ourselves and others. These words came centuries after Qoholeth, but we have them to help us cope:

"Come to me all who are weary and are overburdened and I will give you rest. Shoulder my Yoke and learn from me, for I am gentle and humble in heart and you will have rest for your soul. Yes my Yoke is easy and my burden light." (Matt 11:28–30)

Chapter Two

Exile on Main Street

The Mystery of Suffering

SUFFERING consists in a feeling of loss, injury or desire, be it physical or spiritual. At all levels of human existence it constitutes a religious problem in so far as it imposes on the sufferer various questions.

How do I escape suffering? Why me? How does suffering come to me?

Some religions, e.g. Hinduism and Buddhism, arose from the efforts to overcome suffering: in so far as suffering is rooted in desire, desire has to be obliterated. These religions witness the ever-present question, 'Why suffering?' and, 'What must I do in the face of suffering and sorrow?' Job is innocent and desires to be vindicated; in this lies much suffering.

In Israel of the Old Testament the problem of suffering became more apparent as they developed mono-theism. Israel recognised its election in the covenant which promised material blessings, or curses, as fitting recompense for their response to, or lack of the covenant. (Dt 28–30) But however much the straightforward measure of good rewarded, evil punished (*Psalms* 1,23: *Proverbs* 22,4) might be valid for small communities, experience showed such a system just did not correspond to the lived experience in Israel. God was seen as employing suffering medicinally to bring Israel and individuals back to their senses. (Am 4, Dt 8:16, Ex 20:20, Ps 81) After conversion, suffering might purify the covenant. (Ps 38; Sax 13:8)

At times, however, the promised reward seemed too long postponed or the amount of suffering disproportionate to the sin committed. (Ps 13, Is 35:17, Jer 12:4) Job referred innocent suffering to the mystery of God, who not only created the Universe's wonders, but also ruled over Behemoth and Leviathan symbols of cosmic evil. Sadly, appeal to mystery does not answer rational sufferings.

Apparently undeserved sufferings were explained by the sense of corporate personality, a perception of social reality through which the individual was understood as a representative and, at the same time, a member of the group; for suffering and joy, human beings share each other's fate. God's curse can extend to three or four generations, while his blessings can continue for a thousand generations. (Ex 20:5; Dt 5:9) We can see the sin of Adam and Eve in this perspective. Now, if all must suffer for one person's sin, inversely one can suffer for the sins of all, so the several songs testify. (e.g. Is 53:4–12) This solution of life after death was developed in late prophetic and sapient literature. (Dn 12:2ff, Wisd 3:1–12:5)

In our time there is still to be heard protest against God. Christianity has proclaimed a God who cares for each individual, (Mtt 10:28–31) and in his love 'makes the sun rise on the evil and the good, and sends rain on the righteous and the unrighteous'. (Mtt 5:44) 'But how,' many ask, 'can God be a loving Father if so many of his little ones, so many innocent children, suffer horribly?' Job carried the cries of the suffering, those who suffer innocently, to the heart of God. We are not given answers to so many questions, but Job compliments Qoheleth. Qoheleth spoke for those who struggle. Job speaks for himself and those who suffer. He finds himself all alone in the world. God does come, but only appears late in the story. Job does not provide solutions to life's problems but, on speaking out, he restores dignity to those afflicted by suffering; his word is a statement, that these people do suffer innocently but still belong.

Book of Job

The *Book of Job* resembles more the form of a drama than that of history book. The name of Job as well as the places associated with him and his comforters serve to balance the dramatic effect. In biblical tradition, Job was one of the venerable ancient, along with Noah and Daniel (Ez 14:14,20). Uz, the land where Job lives, is a poetic mythical land. Dermot Cox OFM suggests the word 'Oz' could just as well do. The author wished to locate the protagonists in exotic locations. Job is one of the sons of the East, a title that conjures up images of the Wise One in the time of Solomon.

Dermot Cox, in his commentary on Job, sees it as belonging to the theatre of the absurd. One is confronted by one's experience, and the feeling produced is a feeling of absurdity in the face of reality. The drama involves the reader. Job's experience of suffering can strike a chord with the reader who might have his/her own share of suffering. The voices of those who will not listen are there, but they are ultimately dismissive of the person suffering. So much of the drama cries out to God for some relief, but for a very long time God remains silent. Ultimately He does enter the drama. The very presence of God brings about a change. Job is restored to his wealth, and the comforters go away ashamed. The drama, the poetry and the dialogue involve us and give us a perspective on our sufferings. We are led to explore the 'common wisdom' of our times and come to a new relationship with God.

The drama involves us in this quest – helping us explore our own brokenness, giving a voice to our pain and isolation, and helps us 'hope against hope'. This is the power of story and we find something of ourselves by entering the drama. This is the journey ahead in the meditation of Job.

The Prologue (1:1–2:13) and the Epilogue (42:7–17) are in prose form, while the central book is in poetry. These contain events of happiness, disaster and restoration. The opening section (1:1–2:13) consists of six scenes in which Job loses his property, friends, family and personal health in sequence. The story's perspective alternates between heaven and earth in order to show us, unknown to Job, that what happens on earth to Job is a result of the debate between God and the adversary (Satan). Satan here is not meant as a proper name in our sense of the word 'Satan'. Whatever Job loses is to be restored, but later (42:7–17).

The main body of the text consists of extended dialogues between Job and his three friends (3:1–37:24), which precede the discourse of Elihu (32:1–37:40). Then God addresses Job from the whirlwind (38:1–42:6). Now let us enter the drama proper.

Pictures of Job

Ezechiel mentions Job alongside Noah and Daniel as a paragon of righteousness. (Ez 14:12–20) We come to hear of the patience of Job in James (5:10–11)—here it is mentioned in the context of Job's long suffering and perseverance. The term 'patience of Job' is used by many today, yet the pictures we get of Job from the book are at odds with this. I think Job would be amused at the irony of the situation. 'Job the patient' is the hero of the prose frame of the book, but 'Job the impatient', 'Job the rebel' is the central figure of the poetic dialogue that makes up the heart of the book. 'Job the patient' withstands all the calamities inflicted on him to test his sincerity, and is finally rewarded by redoubled prosperity. This is in accordance with the traditional world view of the time before Job, but the world was fast changing. The shock of the Exile, and post-exilic crises of faith, had heralded a more troubled generation. The hard questions this led to are lived out by the impatient Job in his disclosures. The dialogues contain much response and reaction, but the arguments do not run along predictable lines.

The background of the dialogue is established in Chapters One and Two. Job is introduced. He is a 'blameless and upright man who fears God and shuns evil'. (1:1) His wealth and family are described in numbers, typifying abundance: seven sons and three daughters, seven thousand small cattle and three thousand camels. The happiness of the family is shown by the constant parties held by the children. Job's scrupulousness is shown by his sacrifice on behalf of the children lest they blaspheme God in their hearts. (1:5)

In the next movement of the drama we are led to the divine court. This is to involve the reader in the drama. We are the ones being addressed. We now see what Job cannot see. God singles out Job for praise to one who is of the court of God and is called the adversary (some translators use the term 'Satan'— but this is not understood as our idea of Satan). The adversary chides God for protecting Job. He recommends depriving Job of his possessions and seeing what Job will do then. God accepts the challenge and the adversary goes to complete his task. (1:6–9)

The third movement shows us a gathering at a party in the house of the eldest son. (1:13) A chain of events comes to crush Job, destroying his family and possessions yet 'in all this Job did not sin nor offer any insult to God'. (1:22)

The fourth scene takes us up to the Court of Heaven; here the adversary wants still more. He asks that Job's body be afflicted; God agrees. This picture of God is hard to digest—but he is one of the figures of the drama and opens the door for a clearer vision of God to emerge. God does ask that Job's life be preserved. Job is in agony when the adversary strikes and his wife urges him to curse God and die. (2:9) Job replies: 'If we take happiness from God's hand, must we not take sorrow too.' And in all his misfortune Job uttered no sinful word. (2:10)

The last movement in the drama sees the entry of Job's three friends. They have come from afar to comfort Job. The drama is set up. The patient Job is about to give way to the impatient Job of the dialogues. The author heightens the feeling of tension by telling us that the three friends, Eliphaz of Teman, Bibdad of Shuah, and Zophar of Naamath, kept company with him for seven days, but then Job moves centre stage. The scene is set.

But Job goes on a savage outburst. He begins:

'may the day perish when I was born

and the night that told of a boy conceived
may that day be darkness
may God on high have no thought of it
may no light shine on it' (3:2–5)

Job is crushed by a deep feeling of sadness and of being
alone. Modern thinkers might use the term 'absurd' to describe
Job's position. He is lost and alone, and things are not making
sense.

The outburst takes the friends by surprise; they had come to
commiserate and encourage, not to participate in anything that
smacked of rebellion against God. Eliphaz takes the stage
(Chapter 4–5) he reminds Job of the way he looked after victims
of misfortune, and gently chides him for breaking down under
his own calamity; he quotes the traditional wisdom of his time.
No innocent man was ever wiped out. He repeats a revelation
that came to him in thought-filled visions of the night. (4:13)
Man is too weak to be innocent before God, yet he knows,
from what we saw in the beginning, that Job was praised by
God, so Eliphaz is actually the one who is setting himself
against God as a zealot; but, in his blind adherence to what he
has learned, he is the one who is hurting Job and contradicting
God. Job is not to know what we know, and the words of
Eliphaz fall on Job as hammer blows.

Eliphaz tells Job that 'man is born to trouble, as sparks fly
upwards'. (5:7) It is a lucky man that God disciplines; if the man
accepts it and repents, he has a good hope of being healed and
living prosperously, coming to a ripe old age. Eliphaz belonged
to a certain age and time, but his mean spirit is to be found in all
ages. He was not humble, and he claimed that all he had said
had been proved by experience, but Job had his own experience
too, and Eliphaz had no right to judge him.

The form of the first exchange sets the tone for the dialogue
section of the book. Job screams out his death wish with
passion, becoming the spokesman for all the troubled on the
earth. Eliphaz's carefully modulated reply sets the subsequent

pattern for the friends' replies. Most of the themes of the friends' arguments are included in Eliphaz's speeches: man's worthlessness before God, man's ignorance, the happiness of the penitent and their claim to possess wisdom greater than Job's. Only the wicked suffer and the good prosper. Job knows his truth and he will not compromise this with a lie.

Job enters the fray. If this were a boxing match, then the time for sorting each other out is over, and now the protagonists go at each other full heartedly and no feelings are spared.

Job spoke next. He said:

"If only my misery could be weighed,
and all my ills be put on the scales:
But they outweigh the sands of the seas:
what wonder then if my words are wild?
The arrows of the Shaddai stick fast in me,
my spirit absorbs their poison,
God's terrors stand against me in array.
Does not a wild donkey bray when it finds soft grass
or an ox ever love when its fodder is in reach.
Can tasteless food be taken without salt,
or is there flavour in the white of an egg?
The very dishes which I cannot stomach,
these are my diet in my sickness,
Oh may my prayer find fulfilment,
may God grant me hope!
May it please God to crush me!
to give His hand free play and do away with me!
This thought, at least would give me comfort." (6:1–10)

Job turns against his friends. Perhaps at this stage it would be better to use the more cynical expression 'comforters'. He has found neither friendship nor comfort in them.

The only relief anyone can get in life are his wages and sleep at night; Job has found this is not so. All he finds is suffering.

He wonders how come life is so short and full of suffering it's absurd! He is cynical in his parody of the Psalms. Psalm 8 reads: 'What is man that you are mindful of him, mortal man that you take care of him.' (8:4) In Job this becomes:

"What is man that you make so much of him,
subjecting him to your scrutiny,
that morning after morning you should examine him
and at every instant test him?
Will you ever take your eye off me
long enough for me to swallow my spittle." (7:17–19)

Job would prefer if God would leave him in peace, and let him go away and die in peace. Job does not feel held or loved by God.

Enter Bildad; Job's anger and impatience impel him to come forward and teach Job a thing or two. Slowly but surely Job is finding himself removed from people and from God. He cannot understand what God has done, and his comforters are not listening to his pain; they are now adding to it. "Will the almighty pervert justice?" asks Bildad, and proceeds to tell Job that the death of his children came about because of their sins. Job had prayed while they partied, so he is the subject of a low-blow from Bildad.

People who are right, or believe themselves to be right, justify what they say or do from the perspective of being 'right'. Religious fanatics have always done so. Their gross inhumanity and destruction of good people does not deter them. Bildad strides onto the stage with words which are violent and sickening. Job ought to supplicate God, rather than dare to assert a claim against him. He quotes with ease the ancient sages. He comes forth with his little bit of wisdom. He says there is nature's law that plants wither without water, so the curse of the godless leads to doom. (Bildad was not actually an intellectual colossus.) God will not repudiate the blameless or support the wicked; hence, if Job repents, a joyous future, better than his past, is in store from him.

Job comes back and looks at his two adversaries. He takes their words, 'Can mortals be acquitted by God?' (4:17) 'Will the almighty pervert justice?' (8:3) These questions come from the traditional covenant piety, but now Job cuts loose. 'Man cannot win a suit against God!' (9:2) God indeed works wonders—a generous agreement with Eliphaz—but mainly in displays of his destructive power in nature—turning the tables on Eliphaz after seeming to agree with him—Job is angry but not alone. He has lost his old vision of God; his old relationship with God is over. He cannot see God; what he learned about God is now inadequate to guide him through his pain. His comforters are cruel and judgmental. Job is down and out and they reject him: 'Oh, such an obvious sinner!' 'Why can't he just repent and be done with it?' Job will not abandon himself to these friends, and a world view he now knows to be false. He cannot find God and has many questions about innocent suffering. There is only One that can answer. Job cannot make God answer, only God can be God. It is an extraordinarily lonesome place for Job to be.

Job continues in legal terms. Job denounces God's disregard of his rights. He accuses God of trying to terrify him into confusion. Even if Job could plead, he would find his own words twisted against him contrary to Bildad's assertion, God indiscriminately destroys the innocent and the guilty, 'he wounds me much for no reason'. (9:17) Ironically Job has hit upon the truth here. If God would allow him, Job would demand of Him a bill of indictment. He would charge Him with unworthy conduct, He strikes his creature while smiling on the wicked. He searches for Job's sin, even though He knows Job is not guilty—this is as we remembered in the beginning.

He sustained Job through the years, only to cut him down with a wondrous display of power. (Themes from Psalm 139 are sarcastically re-used here, a trick of Job's to hit at his enemies and their wisdom.)

Zophar has yet to come in, and in Chapter 11 he enters.

With him there is patience and kindness. He denounces Job's self-righteousness. He speaks as one close to God. Such people have an aura of other-worldliness about them, and look with disdain upon other mere mortals. When Jesus spoke he did not have much time for such people. Zophar goes on that if God would answer Job, then God would show him his ignorance. In part, God has treated Job better than he deserves. God's purpose is unfathomable.

"Can you claim to grasp the mystery of God,
to understand the perfection of Shaddai?
It is higher than the heavens: what can you do?
It is deeper than Sheol: What can you know?"

He is utterly dismissive of Job and therefore all who suffer. He speaks as one who is close to God, yet all he can do is to lead people forever away from God. Zophar is a pathetic figure. Job should pray to God and remove his iniquity. Then he will enjoy the hopes, the light, the peace and the sound sleep of the righteous.

Each of the three friends has had his say. Job now comes back even stronger in Chapter 12–14. Goaded by Bildad, he mockingly acknowledges their monopoly of wisdom, but then adds emphatically that he himself is no less wise. Sarcastically looking at Zophar's celebration of God's boundless wisdom, Job invokes the dumb creatures of the sky, sea and earth.

"The creeping things of earth will give you lessons
and the fishes of the sea will tell you all.
There is not one such creature but will know
this state of things is all of God's own making.
He holds in his power the soul of every tiny thing
and the breath of each man's body." (12:8–10)

A nasty combination of words illustrating how little thought his comforters put in their words, and how much damage can be done by a non-critical use of words. Job here sarcastically turns their words on their heads. I doubt very much if the 'comforters' were going to question fish about the mysteries of the Universe!

In this context, the stock praise of God that He 'uncovers deep things out of darkness, brings deep gloom to light' (12:22) suggests, for Job, that he takes the lid off the forces of death and chaos, allowing them to surface and overcome order. As for the comforters, Job turns once again on them. They ascribe false values to God to justify their position. Job does not tell God how to be God, but he will stand up to Him because he knows he is innocent, and, if God is God, then God will recognise his integrity. There lies a deep faith in Job behind the rebellion and hurt he feels. These feelings must be acknowledged, honoured and expressed. Job is putting words on the experience of pain, and carrying these wounds and the wounds of all who suffer innocently to the heart of God, who for now is silent.

Job continues:

"let him kill me if he will. I have no other hope
than to justify my conduct in his eyes" (Job 13:15)

The child of light is soon disillusioned when he realises his vulnerability to God's terror. Again he asks to be informed of his sin, to be allowed to talk with God. (13:20–23, also 6:24,10:2) Again he complains against God's enmity, wonders at his petty handling of events, and his persecution of a 'driven leaf'. (13:25) He implores God to ease his pain, to let him live out his term in peace, because men once cut down can have no more hope but to sleep in Sheol. Job does not believe in an afterlife and this helps to concentrate the all-pervading darkness.

Job however does not stop there to accept the idea of Sheol without thought. He has already brought the problem of innocent suffering centre-stage, and allowed himself to question former ideas of God and Wisdom. He was not just speaking for himself to God, but he becomes a voice for all the oppressed. Then he looks at the idea of Sheol and extends the boundaries of thought yet again. These questions pave the way for belief in the afterlife, and in the Resurrection of Jesus who would show that our life is not in vain.

"If only you would hide me in Sheol
and shelter me there until your anger is past
fixing a certain day for calling me to mind
for once a man is dead can he come back to life"
(Job 14:13–14)

Job is very despondent. Here the first round of dialogues ended. When the first round began Job had rejected life but now he has moved on. In his rebellion he has come to cling to life and also paved the way for a new relationship with God. Job rebelled against his rebellion. Lamentations, anger, despair, and hope succeeded each other in waves. The 'comforters' are stung by Job's challenge to their concept of the moral order. They turned to scolding, harsh words, one more harsh than the other. Eliphaz begins by saying that Job might be a sinner, Bildad suggests his children died for their sins but Zophar kindly tells Job he is getting less than he deserves; yet each are optimistic that all will be well if Job acknowledges his sin and repents. Though they provide no comfort for Job, by blackening his character they end up by shaking him out of his despair and kindle in him the desire to set the record straight. Job would prefer to be a dead lion unlike his counterpart Qoheleth. (Ecc 9:4)

Round Two and Eliphaz struts the stage again. He chides Job for mocking his friend's counsel. Is Job's wisdom personified?

"Were you born before the mountain?" (15:7)

This re-echoes *Proverbs* 8:25. Eliphaz asks does Job have a monopoly of wisdom? (12:2–3) Job's ridicule exposes the nasty side of Zophar 'why are we thought of as brutes?' (18:3)—with 'reproof that insults me'. (20–30) Zophar is tragically blind to what he does himself. Eliphaz mockingly sets Job up. One would think that Job has listened to God's counsel, when in fact it was to Eliphaz that insight into man's true condition was given in the night vision. (15:14–16 re-echoes what we heard in 4:17–21.)

This theme, briefly touched upon previously, is elaborated at length throughout the second round of the friends' speeches. Since they cannot persuade Job to withdraw his case against God, his perseverance convinces them that Job is in sin. They try to frighten him into repentance by detailing the punishment of the wicked; they have Job's misfortune in mind when they detail the fate of the wicked. Eliphaz focuses on the tormented person of the wicked man (Chapter 15). Bildad goes back to the end of Job's family.

> "Driven from light into darkness
> he is in exile from the earth,
> without issue or posterity among his own people,
> none to live on where he has lived.
> His tragic end appals the West,
> and fills the East with terror.
> A fate like this awaits every sinful house,
> the house of every man who knows not God."
>
> (18:18–21)

Zophar uses images from the alimentary canal. The ill-gotten gains of the wicked are sweets they try to swallow, but they must vomit or they will turn to poison in them and kill them. (20)

Job appears a bit more down-beat in this section. He comes in with a sadness:

> "How often I have heard you all before!
> What sorry comforters you are!
> Is there never an end to your angry words?
> What a plague your need to have the last word is!"
>
> (16:1–4)

Job is weary of his comforters trying to brow-beat him. He goes on:

"I lived in peace, until he shattered me,
taking me by the neck to dash me to pieces.
He has made me a target for archery
shooting his arrows at me from all sides.
Pitilessly pierces my loins and pours my gall out
                    upon the ground" (16:12–14)

He could overwhelm his comforters by sermonising to them, but his pain is too real to allow him to indulge in this. Job has been afflicted, and this very thought moves him to plead that the wrong done to him be not forgotten.

"Earth does not cover my blood." (16:8)

He speaks of a witness in heaven who will arbitrate between himself and God, but the light soon dims and he is plunged back into despair.

"For the years of my life are numbered,
and I shall soon take the road of no-return." (16:22)

Responding to Bildad and his description of the wicked man's loss of home and kin, Job relates (Chapter 1) how God took away his honour, and how all abandoned him until only his flesh and bones remained attached to him. He implores his comforters for compassion, he cries out for a permanent record of his arguments and consoles himself with the assurance that, although he is forsaken in the present, there will be a redeeming kinsman (in Hebrew 'Go'el') who lives and will justify him. Job still hopes and trusts in this mythical person; he is utterly convinced that, somewhere in the Universe, there has to be one who will stand up for all that is true, all that is good, and all that is just.

"This I know: that my Avenger lives
and he, the last, will stand on earth." (19:23)

In his reply to Zophar (Chapter 21), Job bids his comforters be silent and listen to something that might be difficult for them, and he would show them something that would silence them. Job confronts them with the real situation of the wicked. Contrary to what they have said, the wicked live long lives, do quite well for themselves, and are surrounded by the blessings of children. They die without pain. Job wonders what sort of judge distributes well-being and misfortune according to such a standard? Even in death, the wicked are honoured. The aura of sadness is inescapable here; like Qoheleth, Job uses the test of wisdom by reality and experience. In the light of this test, the Old ideas of God are totally wanting. Job's misery is plumbing new depths, but where is God?

In round two of the dialogue , the 'comforters' dwelt one-sidedly on the punishment of the wicked, intending Job to see in the wicked a mirror of himself. What they succeeded in doing was to move him to look at his suffering and, in reaction to the comforters' emphasis, the success of the wicked and the plight of the innocent who suffer.

Eliphaz signals the start of round three. He is not now shackled by any effort at being civilised. He asks a profound question of Job and, indeed, of the reader. The stage is being set because the questions asked by both sides cannot be answered by any side. Eliphaz asks:

"Can a man be of any use to God
when even the wise man's wisdom is
of use only to himself?
Does Shaddai derive any benefit from your
integrity, or profit from your blameless conduct?"

(22:1–3)

It is a question that can be reformulated in such words as: 'Do I belong?' or 'Do I matter?' These questions are a torment. For Eliphaz there is no question of torment, as he does not own the questions he asks and all they imply. For people who find life burdensome, who have learned from life through the medium of sexual, mental, physical, or verbal abuse, the answer is often 'No',—'No, I don't matter, and I don't feel I belong anywhere.' Loneliness is more than a state of mind.

Eliphaz sensed the loneliness in souls that are crushed. The words come as hammer blows to people in loneliness; it is another form of nailing Jesus to the Cross. He was nailed to the Cross of loneliness (14) and cried aloud with His pain. Eliphaz's questions are cruel. His questions cry out to God, like the blood of the innocent, for an answer.

Eliphaz re-doubles the pressure on Job. The answers to his questions apply to a good man. He tells Job that in fact he is wicked, as is obvious from his present condition. To paraphrase him, he is saying:

"You don't matter, even if you were good, which obviously you are not. God does punish the wicked, so be a good boy, and not such an embarrassment, and repent. Then all will be well."

Job replies in a soliloquy. (Chapters 23–24) Yes, he would like to find God, not in order to repent, but to argue his case before Him, for he is sure he would be cleared; but God is nowhere to be found. He would emerge as pure gold from a test, and God knows it; yet God is cruel to him. A list of crimes committed by the wicked now appears, mixed in with a description of the downtrodden, and ending with a bitter and cutting reproach: 'Yet God remains deaf to their appeal.' (24:12) Job springs back to life now and says at the end of the soliloquy:

"Is this not so? Who can prove me a liar, or show that my words have no substance?" (24:25)

Here is the answer to Eliphaz: 'People *do* matter.'

Eliphaz had to hear this from the loneliest and simplest person in the world: not only for Eliphaz, but for others in their time and generation, who would deny the rights of the individual. In Eliphaz's case it is doubly important for him to hear this, because he represents himself as standing for God.

His arrogance ill-becomes a man of God. Job is fighting back, not just for himself but for all victims.

Bildath's third speech is short and does not add to the debate:

"Could any man ever think himself innocent,
   when confronted by God?
Born of a woman how could he ever be clean?" (25–4)

The less said the better.

Job now makes a statement in anger against his tormentors, and against all who pretend to care, but are mean-minded, behind a veneer of being 'correct'.

"To one so weak, what a help you are,
   for the arm that is powerless, what a rescuer!
What excellent advice you give the unlearned,
   never at a loss for a helpful suggestion!
But who are they aimed at, these speeches of yours,
   and what spirit is this that comes out of you?" (26:1–4)

The tormentors can be in no doubt that the dialogues are now over. They are doomed to repeating themselves, and Job can mimic their pieces for them. The dialogue is ended, and one protagonist remains, who can bring the drama to its conclusion, but he still remains silent. Zophar—thoughtfully—opts out of making any intervention in Round Three. Job realised that Zophar is not coming forward, and tells us that God has deprived him of all justice. (27:2) He affirms his blame-lessness against his friend's vilification. He will hold on to this integrity as long as he lives. He advises his friends to stop talking the nonsense that their own experience contradicts. (27:12)

He taunts Zophar, mimicking what he might have spoken. Job barks back to Zophar's speech in 20:29. Job gives this reply with an oath invoking, paradoxically: 'God who has deprived me of Justice.' (27:2)

He goes on:

"This is the fate that God assigns to the wicked,
the inheritance that the violent receive from Shaddai,
Though he may have many children, it is put to the
sword, his descendants will never have enough to eat.
Plague will try those he leaves behind him,
and their widows will have no chance to mourn them."

(27:13–16)

Zophar finds his words coming back at him and this gives them a hollow ring. Job holds on to his integrity. Job then leads to a sublime poem on wisdom (Ch.28). He speaks of the wisdom by which the world is governed, by which the meaning of events is locked. Man knows how to get precious ore from the earth, and he can conquer the most daunting of obstacles to recover the ore. Yet, he does not have a map to the source of wisdom:

"'It is not in me' says the Abyss;
'Nor here' replies the Sea.
It cannot be bought with solid gold,
nor paid for with any weight of silver" (Job 28:13–15).

Death has only heard a rumour of this wisdom. God alone, who stands above the Abyss, can comprehend it. This poem seems out of context in many ways, but it does serve to allow God to take centre-stage. The whole of the drama has been crying out to allow God to speak. Job seems to be saying to his comforters, 'Abandon your false doctrine, it is a reproach to you and will not gain God's favour.' These are Job's last words to his 'friends'.

Now one would expect silence, or the entry of God Himself, but enter the upstart Elihu. Elihu takes the stage now. He is like an uninvited guest, dark, and with a frightening arrogance. He has seen the three comforters fall, now he is prepared to throw his lot in. The Young Pretender! He excuses his intervention by citing the importance of his elders. Though insisting he will not repeat what has been said (32:14) he does drag us over familiar ground. Thus, to Job's charge that God does not answer, Elihu replies that man, through dreams and illness, comes to see these as God's messengers to call one to repent. He counters Job's complaint of God's injustice by affirming that the sole ruler of the earth can do no wrong. Elihu argues that the good and evil that men do cannot affect God, but only other people. This is a harsh, cold view of God, and indeed a punitive one, but Elihu does suggest that God punishes the wicked. Elihu's speech opens with an interpretation of the suffering of the virtuous as disciplinary, and concludes with a rhapsody to God's greatness, as seen in the phenomena of rain, thunder and lightening. Elihu is more advanced in this stage of the argument, but one is left with the feeling that nothing of substance has been added.

Now, at last, we can move to the next stage of the drama. The very tension of the book has cried out for God to appear, or else turn His face from Job and allow him die in peace.

"Then from the heart of the tempest Yahweh gave Job his
answer. He said:
'Who is obscuring my designs
with his empty-headed words?
Brace yourself like a fighter;
now it is my turn to ask questions and yours to inform
me.
Where were you when I laid the earth's foundations?
Tell me, since you are so well-informed!
Who decided the dimensions of it, do you know?
Or who stretched the measuring line across it?
What supports its pillars at their bases?" (38:1–6)

The tone of the drama now shifts: God has entered, and addresses Job. In one sense, Job has his answer—yes, he was right; the individual, and individual suffering, did matter. God Himself comes to address the one who cried out to Him, and a new relationship, I--Thou, is born.

This new relationship is the keystone for Job's new life. He was right, after all, to leave behind his old wisdom, and the face of God that sustained that wisdom. The new relationship takes off with God exchanging roles with Job. Up to this, Job has demanded answers from God; now God sets unanswerable questions to Job about the foundations of the Universe. Does Job know anything about the fashioning and operation of the cosmic elements—earth, sea, the underworld and darkness? Has he knowledge of, or control of, the celestial phenomena of snow, hail, thunder and lightening, or the constellations? From these, God turns to the animals, the lions, the raven whose young cry to God for food, mountain goats, whose birth God only attends, the wild ass, the wild ox, the ostrich, the war horse, the eagle and the falcon. The God of Job celebrates each act of creation, and products of this act in themselves.

Job is now different. He is in a different relationship with God, and to God's questions he replies:

"My words have been frivolous: what can I reply?
I had better lay my finger on my lips.
I have spoken once... I will not speak again;
more than once... I will add nothing." (40:3–5)

Job could be saying to God, 'How can I answer You, when You have the upper hand?' But it could be that, in his new-found relationship, he is struck by the mystery of God, and his questions about suffering are caught up in mystery. God comes back again asking Job would he condemn Him, so that Job would prove himself right (40:8). Job has railed against the prosperity of the wicked, attributing it to Divine indifference or cruelty. God uses much the same style in His arguing as Job did. He invites Job to try his hand at making things right, if he could:

"Has your arm the strength of God's?
Can your voice be as loud?

If so, assume your dignity, your state,
robe yourself in majesty and splendour.
Let the spate of your anger flow free;
humiliate the haughty at a glance!" (40:9–11)

If he can do better, then God will sing Job's praises. Once
again, Job's ignorance and importance are involved to disqualify
him from doing too much. Only someone who understands the
vastness of God's projects can sit in judgement of them.

I remember a distinction made by the French existentialist
thinker, Gabriel Marçel. He spoke of the difference between a
problem and a mystery. A problem—e.g. a mathematical one—is
something we can try and solve. We can somehow stand outside
it. But we can't approach mystery in the same way. We are
involved in mystery and we are not outside it.

Job is learning this about the mysteries he has come across:
innocent suffering, creation, and the plans and designs of God.
Really to show Job his powerlessness, God speaks of Behemoth
and Leviathan; this shows that man no longer has the same
control as original man had in Paradise. Behemoth is a land
animal, is powerful, and his bones are like metal bars. Leviathan
is a denizen of the waters, and flames and smoke come from
him. The effect of this parade is to excite amazement before the
mystery of creating, the mystery of life. God's governance
cannot be judged by its manifestation in human society alone.
No one can comprehend God, and his works defy any narrow
meaning. They belong to the region of Marçel's mystery. Now
comes the crunch: to condemn His supervising of man's affairs,
because it does not conform to human conceptions of reason
and justice, is improper.

Job was judged by these false standards, and he rejected the
judgements he received as wrong; and here, with God's sight,
Job's fundamental intuition was right. A new relationship with
God was called for. Job's God is more personal than one
presented by his comforters. Their God was disinterested, and
one for Whom people didn't matter. Job rejected this, and thus

allowed God to enter a new relationship with him; but, not all the questions Job asked were answered. The sheer force of mystery would not allow this. Job now submits unequivocally. (42:2–6) He confesses his ignorance and presumptuousness in speaking of matters beyond his knowledge. Now that he has not only heard of God—i.e. known of Him by tradition—but also sees Him, he rejects what he formerly maintained and is consoled, 'being mere dust and ashes'. (V.6) The adversary has lost his wager. Throughout his trial, Job had no regret for having lived righteously. He thus gave the lie to the adversary's boast that his virtue depended on reward.

We are now winding down from the high drama, and the dramatis personæ are about to leave the stage. The Epilogue (42:7–17) relates Job's rehabilitation. God reproaches Eliphaz, the chief representative of 'the friends'. Job bears them no malice. God chides them for not having spoken rightly about Him, as Job did. Job here re-echoes what Job said in 13:7–10.

"Do you mean to defend God by prevarication
and by dishonest argument
and taking sides with this
appoint yourselves as His advocates?"

God defends himself from being a moral accountant. This was the way in which the friends interpreted Job's sufferings as punishment for sin, and Job ascribed injustice to God. Since the prayer of the injured, on behalf of those who injured him, is the most effective intercession (cf. Gen. 20:7,17), God orders the friends to seek Job's intervention in prayer on their behalf. This becomes the act of mutual reconciliation, and Job is restored to his material possessions; his possessions are doubled (rem: Bildad's promise), and his children equal in number to those he lost. Job dies at a ripe old age, a symbol of God's blessing.

The Mystery of Suffering in Job and Jesus

Suffering comes to people in different forms. For Job it came in personal tragedy, sickness and anguish of mind. The categories covering these would be: trauma, grief and post traumatic stress disorder, and mental illness.

Trauma and grief come as a result of bereavement, of violence of whatever kind (physical, emotional, psychological, sexual), grief accompanies trauma, and is a dark valley to go through. Post-traumatic stress disorder is what remains after the trauma is passed; it is the emotional fallout that is left behind afterwards. Illness is another form of suffering; it changes one's whole viewpoint in life. Before the onset of serious illness, one's world view can be reasonably content, and one can find oneself coping to a certain extent. The sudden onset of illness comes as a shock to the system. The sudden finding of how powerless one is, is a shock, and one is brought face to face with things and values that went unquestioned for years. One can be weakened and brought to fear. That is the position of Job; in this light we can see how cruel his comforters were. Depressive illness often follows.

One can react to one's environment and come to see the world as hostile. Job cursed the day he was born (3:1–5) and God as the one who deprived him of justice (27:3). Job lived out in himself the fullness of all these disorders. All around us we see the same story acted out in human beings. We have the innocent victims of war and terrorism, we have the grief of the old who are abandoned by family, we have those who carry crippling emotional baggage from the past, and this poisons their life. Job helps initiate us to see that the 'Why' of suffering is a mystery that does not admit to any easy answer, but his new relationship with God points to the fact that the cry of the one who suffers touches the heart of God. As Christians, we go one step further and know that the definite victory is God's, but we willingly see this victory in the new earth and the new heroes, where there is no more mourning, nor crying, nor pain (Rv 21). The sufferer who lives out this mystery is already, while on earth, a prophet of true life; the life that does not pass away.

This leads me to stand before the Christ-figure. Then is it possible not to believe that God is love when He suffers as I do? Job would say, "I do not know why I suffer," whereas a Christian might say, "Jesus died for us, and was raised to life for my justification."

Our relationship with God is healed, and this will ultimately lead to the healing of all wounds that hurt us. Christ did not come in order to explain suffering, but to fill it with his presence, to share it, to transfigure it by giving us his spirit in which to bear our suffering. The face of suffering is the face of the crucified Christ. Job helps us bring our brokenness to the heart of God, who show us He is not deaf to our cries.

Emmanuel Mounier, journalist and founder of personalist philosophy, gives the following testimony when he learned that, as a result of encephalitis, his first child would remain forever in a mysterious darkness of the mind. The suffering of the innocent one did not repel him, but defended his love.

"No, this cannot be chance or accident... Someone came, he was important, and this is not a misfortune... There was nothing to do but remain silent before this young mystery that gradually filled us with joy... I felt that in approaching this little voiceless bed I was approaching an altar in a sacred place where God was speaking through a sign... I have never had the spirit of prayer so intensely as when my hand spoke of things to the forehead that gave no answer; as when my eyes dared look at this distracted gaze that looked far, far beyond me, in an act related to the gaze that sees much better than a gaze. It is a mystery, and one which can only be a mystery of goodness, or, dare I say it? a grace, too burdensome a grace. A living victim among us, speechless like the host, radiant like the host ... When so many innocents are torn in pieces, so many innocents trampled under foot, this child, who was immolated day after day, was perhaps

our presence to the horrors of the age... From morning
to evening, let us not think of this evil as something taken
from us, but as something which we give, so that we may
not break faith with this little Christ who is in our midst;
that we may not leave him alone, this little one who
should draw us; that we may not leave his work alone
with Christ... Nothing more resembles Christ than the
innocent who suffer."

A. Beguin, *Mounier et Sa Generation* (1940)

God, then, has not eliminated our suffering. When we, in
our suffering, look to the innocent One who was crucified, we
find we meet God there. Innocent suffering now has the
features of the innocent One who was crucified. St. Paul adds
that:

"the sufferings of this present time are not worth
company with the glory that is to be revealed to us."

(Rom 8:18)

It is possible to conceive of more love than is to be found in
our own suffering world. We look at Christ for this.

Chapter Three

Love is Strong as Death:
The Canticle of Canticles

Title and Date of Composition

THE title in 1:1 *(Song of Songs)* is the Hebrew idiom for superlative. It means 'the greatest song'. It imposes a unity on a collection of poems. The work is ascribed to Solomon as author, because of the appearance of his name in 3:7ff and 5:1ff. Common opinion gives a post-exilic date, although some of the individual poems might have been composed much earlier. It is one of the works chosen for reading at the Passover.

The work is essentially a drama between two main characters. It is dramatic in the sense that there is a dialogue between the following speakers: a woman, a man, and the daughters of Jerusalem. The gender differences are clear in the Hebrew text, but not so clear in the English translations. The main speaker is the woman; the man appears both as shepherd (1:7) and king (1:4,12) by a fiction common in literature of the time.

Several literary forms appear: poems of yearning (1:2–4, 2:14–15), teasing (1:7–8, 2:15), admiration (1:15–2:3, 4:9–5:1, 6:4–7), reminiscence (2:8–113), boast (6:8–10) and description of physical charms (4:1–7, 5:10–16, 7:1–6). They also contain several themes common to all love-literature: love-sickness, obstacles to love, uniqueness, etc.

Both Synagogue and Church agree on a religious interpretation to the *Canticle*. They see the *Canticle* as referring to the love of the Lord for His people, or for the Christian, to the love of Christ for the Church (or the individual soul). This

47

view can be seen in the metaphor of the marriage between the Lord and Israel (Hos 1–3; Is 62:5).

Roland E. Murphy, in his article on the *Canticle of Canticles* in the *New Jerome Biblical Commentary* sees the traditional interpretation as having much to recommend it. Human love should not be seen apart from Divine love, as the biblical symbolism of marriage indicates. Current scholarly opinion holds that the literal sense of the *Canticle* is the expression of human sensual love. This, however, does not exhaust the richness of the *Canticle* but, if anything, enhances it. It recognises that all human love is somehow a share in Divine love. As we hear in 8:6 'human love is the flame of Yahweh'.

The language of the *Canticle* draws images from the atmosphere of the fields: gazelles and hinds, doves and foxes; sheep and goats. The gifts of nature abound: wine and vineyard, cedars and cypresses, figs and pomegranates. The imagery is drawn from many worlds. Persons become transfigured. Love creates a world of its own. Hence we hear about the 'tower of ivory' (7:5) and of 'lips that drip choice myrrh' (5:13). It can be disconcerting to hear of the woman's hair compared to a flock of goats streaming down Mount Gilead. The language here is evocative in this wonderful world of love.

The *Canticle* has theological significance and very human significance. In the Old Testament world, human love was seen as intrinsically good, and even a symbol of Divine love. This fact has often gotten lost and the *Canticle* nearly ignored. But the *Canticle* holds its place proudly. Mutuality and fidelity between lovers, the seriousness of the relationship, the devotion to each other, clearly emerge from the *Canticle*. It is widely held that the sages of Israel are responsible for the preservation and transmission of the *Canticle* because they recognised the value of human love (*df* Prov 5:18, 18:22).

Relationships and love properly belong in the eyes of God. The *Canticle* is His world where this is celebrated. Like Job and Qoheleth, some people find difficulty in the *Song of Songs* but it has always troubled people because of a difficulty of some in seeing the holiness of so-called 'purely human love'.

The Heart of the Canticle

I begin my look at the *Canticle*—or the *Song of Songs*—with the following words of the Lover:

"I compare you, my love,
to a mare of Pharaoh's chariots,
your cheeks show fair between their pendants
and your neck with its necklaces.
We shall make you golden earrings
and beads of silver." (1:9–11)

Suddenly the man is present and breaks forth in a celebration of the beauty of the woman, but the imagery is very different from our time. Few women would like to be referred to as a mare, although in the older culture, from which the *Canticle* came, this was a compliment. He addresses her as 'my love', a term of endearment found eight times between 1:6 and 6:4. She is pictured as wearing simple clothing, which he promises to replace with 'ornaments of gold' (v.11).

The dialogue between the two continues:

"I am the rose of Sharon
the lily of the valleys
—As a lily among the thistles
so is my love among the maidens,
As an apple tree among the trees of the overlord,
so is my beloved among the young men,
In his longed for shade I am seated
and his fruit is sweet to my taste." (2:1–4)

Nature is the palace where the two lovers meet and converse. The woman continues the fantasy by describing herself as, 'Spring flowers on the fertile hills of Sharon and in the valleys of Jezreel.' Her love prompts him to correct her description by protesting to her that, compared to her, all other women are as 'thistles' (v.2). She repays the compliment to him by calling him an apple tree, in contrast to other young men, because other trees promise no 'edible fruit' (v.2) she seeks him for his longed-for shade – his shadow – which is ordinarily an image of protection. However, in the ancient Near-East, this image denotes sexual union, which produces sweet fruit (v.3 see also 4:13, 16:8: 11–12). The woman is sick with love:

"Sustain me with raisins
restore me with apples,
for I am sick with love." (2:5–6)

The woman is overwhelmed by her fantasies and by present reality. Both interconnect and interlock throughout the *Canticle*. Here she feels faint and asks for 'raisins' and 'apples', the two foods whose taste or aroma can seem to prevent fainting. They act as a medicine for her, for she is sick with love! The only cure for love-sickness is the presence of the love. Therefore she cries out to be embraced:

"His left hand is under my head
his right hand embraces me." (2:6)

This is a powerful meditation on love. The openness and honesty of the woman are touching. The strong role she takes in the dialogue is not something that one would have expected in a male dominated society, as she lived in ancient Isræl which was male dominated. To stand outside that norm was to place her in a very vulnerable position. Yet she was prepared to take that risk. The strength of her feelings did not discourage her. It is interesting that, in therapy, many people are told to get in touch with their feelings. Many struggle with angry thoughts, with anger itself forgetting to acknowledge other feelings that go for healthy living. One of these is love. The lover and his beloved are consumed by love and are integrating love into their lives. It is from this perspective that they will confront their futures.

The woman continues her fantasies. It is very effective to see how, in the *Canticle* we see a dream-like world where fantasy and reality fuse. The abiding reality is love, which draws sense from a confused world. The bride continues:

"I hear my beloved.
See how he comes,
leaping on the mountains
bounding over the hills.
My beloved is like a gazelle
like a young stag.

"See how he stands
behind our wall.
He looks in at the window
he peers through the lattice." (2:8–10)

She begins by describing her emotional reaction to the voice of her beloved (v.8). His gazing at her is an expression of his desire for intimacy. Her beloved's desire is like the rich Palestinian spring:

"for lo, the winter is far past,
the rains are over and gone.
The flowers appear on the earth.
The season of glad songs has come. (2:11–133)

Then, as she reveries about union with her beloved, there enters a sudden shift for the anticipated union. We come to a picture of physical separation of the loves (3:1ff).

"On my bed at night, I sought him
whom my heart loves.
I sought but did not find him.
So I will rise and go through the City;
in the streets and the squares
I will seek him when my heart loves

... I sought him but did not find him.
The Watchmen came upon me
on their rounds of the City:
Have you seen him whom my heart loves?" (3:1–5)

She had just spoken about her beloved as being with the flocks all night, now she searches for him in the city. This is the surreal effect achieved in the song. The whole effect is that of a dream sequence, or a stream of conscientiousness. The path of love is marked with difficulties, loneliness and blind alleys. In her desperation she seeks help from the watchmen of the city, but gets no satisfaction. Contrast this with a later loss:

"I opened to my beloved
but he had turned his back and gone!
My heart failed at the plight,
I sought him but could not find him,
I called on him but he did not answer.
The Watchmen came upon me
as they made their rounds of the City.
They beat me, they wounded me,
they took away my cloak,
they who guard the ramparts." (5:6–8)

Then we see a more aggressive reaction for the watcher. They take away the woman's cloak. This is her protection and now she is left exposed to the perils of the night. Her pain a loss, her grief indeed what comes across in these lines at being abandoned.

It is unseemly for a woman to pursue her loved one so openly, and she is open to being misunderstood—as is seen in the cruel treatment by the watchmen. Intimacy and subsequent loss form part of relationships. When John of the Cross wrote his *Dark Night of the Soul,* he would use this imagery, of loss and regaining, as the dark night of senses and of the Soul. Each 'loss' is merely a purification, and leads on to a deeper union than before. In his case, he was referring to the soul before

God. Here we love the love of the Beloved and lover, and how they deepen with each feeling of loss.

The bridegroom addresses the bride with the following words:

"How beautiful you are, my love,
how beautiful you are!
Your eyes, behind your veil,
are doves;
your hair is like a flock of goats
frisking down the slopes of Gilead.
Your teeth are like a flock of shorn ewes
as they come up from the washing.
Each one has its own twin,
no one impaired with another.
Your lips are a scarlet thread
and your words enchanting.
Your eyes, behind your veil,
are halves of pomegranate.
Your neck is the tower of David,
built as a fortress,
hung round with a thousand bucklers,
and each the shield of a hero.
Your two breasts are like two fawns,
twins of a gazelle,
that feed among the lilies." (4:1–5)

Modern commentators refer to this form of praise or lyric as a wasf: a lyric devoted to the praising of the bride or a bridegroom in contemporary Syria wedding ceremonies—see also 5:10–16.

Here the man opens with a description of the physical claims of the woman, and singles out various parts of her body that deserve praise. Her black hair suggests goats in Gilead in the northern Transjordanian plain—not an image that comes readily to a modern reader–but our loves feel free enough to be at home with their own imagery. The breasts of the woman are compared to twin fawns for beauty and grace (cf:2:16, 7:4–16). This is a play on 2:17 where the woman invites him to the mountains (herself). Now he expresses his acceptance of the invitation. Again we move to the *Song's* theme of seeking and finding. Here it is developed by means of language of cantorship, expressed in an indirect way:

> "Before the dawn wind rises,
> before the shadows flee,
> I will go to the mountain of Myrrh,
> to the hill of frankincense.
> You are wholly beautiful, my love,
> and without a blemish." (4:6–7)

The man anticipates ecstatic union with his 'love' as a 'mountain of myrrh' and 'hill of frankincense'—v.6 repeats phrases from 1:13 and 3:6. When he says his love has no blemish, he chooses a word that resonates on a variety of levels – physical, moral, personal – all of which form part of that little thing called love.

In this section, he called the woman 'my bride' (v.8), a term to be found six times between 4:8 and 6:1. He also proclaims that his love is 'all fair' (v.7, In 4:1 and 1:15) the translation 'beautiful' is used in some editions (RSV). The man continues speaking down to v.16 and he also addresses his bride as 'my sister'. In 8:1 she wonders why is her beloved not 'her brother'! These seem strange to us—why should newly-weds wish such a thing? The answer, perhaps, lay in society's view of woman and man, and the tolerated public expression of affection between the two. It was easier for brother and sister to show affection in public. The bridegroom also compares his loved-one to a garden:

> "She is a garden enclosed,
> my sister, my promised bride:

a garden enclosed,
a sealed fountain.
Your shoots form an orchard of pomegranate trees
the rarest essences are yours:
nard and saffron,
calamus and cinnamon,
with all the incense-bearing trees;
myrrh and aloes,
with subtlest odours.

"Fountain that makes the gardens fertile,
well of living water,
streams flowing down from Lebanon." (4:12–16)

She is a garden sealed, that is reserved for him alone. The wide variety of precious and fragrant fruit cannot be found in any one place, yet are here used to highlight his beloved. They hide the minute he comes to the garden (v.18) and in 5:1 he tells us that he comes to the garden, and he possesses her—symbols of spices, honey and wine. Each loss brings a more forward and intimate loving union. Each trial just leads to our lovers coming to an even deeper union. The sense of intimacy overcomes the feelings of loss and abandonment.

The themes of loss and separation are repeated again in the section from 5:2–6:3. In this section, the woman hears the knocking of her beloved on the door, but she delays letting him in, and he goes on. He leaves myrrh (a fragrant spice) on the lock of the door as a sign of his presence. The dream effect is maintained here, and we are caught in this dream-world. This departure causes her to search for him once more. She is humiliated by the watchman (5:7). In the drama that unfolds she begins a dialogue with the daughters of Jerusalem, who want a description of this wondrous being:

"What makes your beloved better than other lovers,
O loveliest of women?
What makes your beloved better than other lovers,

to give us a charge like this?" (5:9)

The effect of the chorus of the daughters of Jerusalem also adds dramatic effect to the dream-like drama. Here they are the wasf which follows where the woman describes the physical charms of her husband (9–16). After this the daughters desire to see this handsome man, but she replies:

"My Beloved went down to his garden
to the beds of spices
to pasture his flocks in the gardens
and gather lilies.
I am my Beloved's and my Beloved is mine.
He pastures his flocks among the lilies." (6:2–3)

Here she is confident that she has lost him fully. The second experience of loss has had the result of deepening her trust in him. Her love has deepened. As if to prove her love is correct, we come upon another wasf uttered by man.

Then, in a passionate outburst, the man expresses his desire for the physical passion of the woman:

"In stature like the palm tree,
its fruit clusters our breasts.
'I will climb the palm tree,' I resolved,
'I will seize its clusters of dates.'
May your breasts be clusters of grapes,
your breath sweet-scented as apples,
your speaking, superlative wine." (7:7–10)

She continues the metaphor of wine in her speech. She invites him to go to the fields with her. The awakening of nature is a recurring theme in the *Song* (cf 2:11–13, 6:11). She wishes he were her brother (8:1) so that she could kiss him publicly with no one thinking ill of her. She would lead him into her mother's house where she would give him 'spiced wine to drink'—a beautiful metaphor for loving. Their union is now complete. They come through the pain of separation, love-sickness, misunderstandings and the lack of tolerance of their world. They have grown in care and mutual understanding and self-giving, and the trials they went through only served to deepen the love they had for each other.

In the confusion of the *Song* we find the following words spoken by the woman:

"Set me like a seal on your heart,
like a seal on your arm.
For love is strong as death,
jealousy relentless as Sheol,
the flash of it is a flash of fire,
a flame of Yahweh himself.

"Love no flood can quench,
no torrents drown." (8:6–7)

These lines suggest a wisdom writer, who put the *Song* into its final form as a way of teaching about the mysterious power that God has given to love. It refers to the thing that moves towards union on every level of interpersonal relationships. We are told 'love is strong as death', that is, it is irresistible. Death can be understood as the power of the underworld. Death is jealous of anything that can take its place in human existence. Love is such a thing. Its flashes are a flash of fire, the flame of Yahweh himself. It withstands many waters—'many waters' can mean any overwhelming trouble. No kind of difficulty can overcome love. No money can buy love.

The conclusion of the *Song* seems to come from different authors and are really appendices. This is the view of the Jerusalem Bible. The speakers in vs.11–12 are difficult to make out. The location 'Baal-human' appears nowhere else in the Bible. The price demanded for each of the keepers is enormous. Possibly this verse was inserted to illustrate the value of love (v.7). In response to this text, the unidentified speaker, probably the man of the song, protests that he has 'my vineyard, my very own' to cater for. This statement reflects the lament of the

woman that she did not keep 'my own vineyard' (1:6). This little
insert at the end seems to be one of the early interpretations of
the poem. It proclaims, once again, the incomparable gift of
love that was expressed in the four maxims above.

Then we come to the final addition:

"You who dwell in the gardens,
my companions, listen for your
voice: deign to let me hear it.
Haste away, my Beloved,
be like a gazelle, a young stag,
on the spicy mountains." (8:13–14)

As in 2:14, the lover asks for a word or song, and she replies
with an invitation similar to that found in 2:17. The *Canticle*
opened with her yearning for his kisses (1:2), now she invites
him to herself—'mountains'. Love involves growth until union
is reached A. Robert, a French biblical scholar, believes that
verse 13 is a prayer addressed to the Lord under the title, *You
who Dwell in the Gardens*. It is a plea to God, as infinite
Wisdom, to instruct His people. Now the 'Beloved' is Yahweh,
the Lord himself as the spouse of Isræl, who offers prayer as
intimate union with Himself. We therefore find, in the final
edited form, that the final author recognised that more than one
message could be given to the lyrics, and we are encouraged to
enter the tent, and seek and find meaning—just as our loves
sought and found love, 'the flame of Yahweh himself'.

There is an element of disunity in the *Canticle*, in the way in
which it dismembers the body, its total disregard for logical
connections. We see this break in logical connections (3:6–11)
where the poet speaks in his own person. There is a description
of the caravan of Solomon:

"What is this coming up from the desert
like a column of smoke,
breathing of myrrh and frankincense
and every perfume the merchant knows?

Here comes Solomon's litter.
Around it are sixty champions."

This is a description of the special ceremonial carriage, accompanied by a select group of ceremonial guards. The impression is that King Solomon functions as a literary 'royal fiction' to disquiet the bridegroom. Yet, here again, the *Song* suddenly breaks off with no definite union between the couple. It has abruptly abandoned the line of thought upon which it embarked. This disunity is very much the lot of the lovers, whose work of integration, and total union and possession, can never fully be climaxed. Constantly, in seeking for unity, they assent differences and distances.

One is a lily (2:2), the other an apple tree (2:3), one is a doe (2:99, 17, 17; 8:14), the other a dove (2:14); the beloved seeks the lover through the streets of the City (3:2, 5:6). He waits impatiently outside her door (5:20), snatching glimpses through the lattice (2:9). Consequently the *Song* has a dramatic quality as the lovers alternately converge and withdraw.

There is no story with a well-defined beginning and end in the *Song*. There is a story in poetic, dramatic form of love relationships, more between closeness and distance, seeking and finding. No relationship comes ready-made, but has to be worked on and deepened with each new experience.

The *Song* lives between reality and dream to show the relationship of the lovers. The flow of the text shows that the course of love does not run smoothly. The dominance and the initiative of the Beloved are among the poem's most astonishing characteristics. In the poem she is aligned with the feminine aspect of divinity—Marvin Pope, in his commentary on the *Song of Songs*, develops this. She is associated with celestial bodies, the land and fertility. In this, she reverses the predominantly patriarchal thought of the Bible. Male power is enthralled by her (ef. the fiction of Solomon in 3:6–11). However the lovers live in a patriarchal world, a male-dominated world. She suffers humiliation in being so adventurous. She is cast out by her family (1:6), despised by shepherds (1:7), beaten by the watchmen (5:7). The lovers can only find or imagine an enclosure, their garden. These images are metaphors for the struggle the couple had to undergo to find acceptance and mutual understanding. They were approaching a partnership of living in a new, more equal but self-giving way, and society would struggle to accept this since at this time women were not seen to be in any way equal to men. Our lovers are aware of these barriers, but they do not accept them as normative to their lives. The Beloved takes the initiative in this.

The New Testament and the Metaphor of God's Love

The *Song of Songs* alludes to a truth that is fundamental to the Christian way of life:

"Love is from God and everyone who lives is a child of God and knows God. Whoever fails to love does not know God, because God is love." (Jn 4:7–8)

St. Paul, in his vision of the Christian message, takes up the same theme. In the letter to the Romans Paul says:

"Love can cause no harm to your neighbour, and so love is the fulfilment of the law." (13:10)

The Beloved, who cries out in the *Song* that 'love is strong as death', finds an echo in Paul's claim, 'Love never comes to an end' (1 Cor 13:8 of Song 8:6). This declaration corresponds with Paul's assertion, again in *Romans*, that:

"neither death nor life, nor angels, nor principalities, nothing already in existence and nothing still to come, nor any power, nor the heights nor the depths, nor any created thing whatever, will be able to come between us and the love of God, known to us in Christ Jesus our Lord" (Romans 8:38–39)

The *Song of Songs* helps make more personal some of the pages of the New Testament. An awareness of the intensity of the woman's search helps highlight such passages as:

"Ask and it will be given to you:
search and you will find,
knock the door will be opened to you."
(Matt 7:7, Heb 11:9–13, cf Sg 3:1–4, 5:2–6)

The witness of the young woman highlights for us that what we seek is the Lord Himself who loves us. We see, too, in the *Book of Revelations* that Jesus is the one, the lover, who knocks at the door, awaiting entrance to our community and to our hearts. (Rev 3:20, cf Sg 8:2)

In the post Resurrection account of the *Gospel of John*, we see Mary Magdalene reflect the disposition of the Beloved in search for the one she loves (Jn 20:17, cf 20:19–23, Jn 2:7).

Both Jewish and Christian scholars have contemplated the *Song of Songs* as an exposition of the love God has for His people. For this reason, Jewish tradition developed the custom of reading the *Song of Songs* on the Sabbath before Passover. In Paul's letter to the Ephesians, we have Paul's reflection on marriage as the symbol of Christ's love for his Church (Eph 5:21–33). This reflects the same tradition. Origen considered the *Song* to be an allegory, both for God's relationship to the Church, and of Christ's relationship to the individual believer. St. Bernard of Clairvaux saw in the *Song* an unparalleled meditation on the union of the soul with God in divine love.

All these, in their different ways, witness to the wealth of spiritual wisdom that is to be found in our lovers' quest: their loving and fidelity. Their love led to the *Canticle of Canticles* and we can share their quest for love.

Love is as Strong as Death and the Vision of John

Nicos Kazantzakis, in his autobiography *Report to Greco*, relates a legend he heard in his native Isle of Crete. The story concerns John the Apostle. John finds himself in contemplation before the Cross; he is caught up in love with the Christ who reveals God's love to us. As he gazes, he sees the face and body of Christ change, taking on the form of men and women from other ages, until all that is left is a cry.

This vision has always touched me. It helps me see that Christ is present in all who suffer, and more, that His love reaches all who suffer in whatever age, whatever time, whatever place. It reaches me, too, in my time. The love of God in Christ is stranger than death, and reaches down across the ages to all. This is something that is hard to take on board on a personal level.

In the face of much of our suffering is personal fear. The fear is that we are somehow judged and not cherished, in any way, by God or humankind; that somehow we are not worth it. This fear can, and does, compound our suffering, but the testimony of the Cross and Resurrection are powerful witnesses to us that our:

> "Love consists in this:
> It is not we who loved God,
> but God loved us and sent His son
> to expiate our sins."   (1Jn 4:10)

The love of God in Jesus was not overcome by darkness, not even by the darkness of death, and is still offered to us today.

Chapter Four

If You See Him Say Hello

PAUL was one of the most dynamic Christians of the early Church. I know that I have looked at Paul with rose-tinted glasses, and have not seen his faults. When people deride St. Paul, I go on the defensive, and continue thus when Paul's mass of contradictions and struggles become obvious. Part of my world-view was shaped by the thought of holy people being so far above and removed from my world that they are completely unreal. It was as if they did not labour under the same sky, make tragic mistakes and hurt each other. St. Luke, in his *Acts of the Apostles*, paints an idyllic picture of the early Church:

> "And all who shared the faith owned everything in common, they sold their goods and possessions and distributed the proceeds themselves according to what each one needed." (Acts 2:44)

This idealised account shows us the ideal to be achieved but, as the rest of the book of the *Acts* makes clear, this only comes about through struggle, human error, and coping with disappointment, especially in the minefield of human relationships. No wonder storms and shipwrecks are such a large part of the *Acts*.

Enter Barnabas

Paul did have difficulty in human relationships; Barnabas was about to enter Paul's life, but they were to break off from each other in a very bitter manner. Barnabas originally came from Cyprus (Acts 4:36) and settled in Jerusalem. He had strong Jewish roots as a Levite (Acts 4:36) and his Hellenistic background in the Jewish diaspora gave him a background similar to Paul's, whose close friend he would become for a while.

Along with Stephen, Barnabas represents the large number of Hellenistic Jews who made their way back to Jerusalem. Luke reminds us that, at the Crucifixion of Jesus, there were many Hellenistic Jews in the city. Barnabas could even be one of these. An early tradition, stemming from Eusebius, says that Barnabas was one of the seventy sent out by Jesus (Luke 10). This is still a matter to be decided by scholars. Barnabas owned land in Jerusalem. His first appearance, in the New Testament, shows him among the earliest converts, selling his little patch of land and giving the proceeds to the Apostles:

"There was a Levite of Cypriot origin called Joseph whom the Apostles surnamed Barnabas (which means son of encouragement). He owned a piece of land and he sold it and he gave the money to the Apostles."

(Acts 4:36:37)

The quotation used here is from the Jewish Bible; Barnabas is a Greek name interpreted by Luke as 'huious parakletos'. This can be translated in various ways, e.g. 'son of consolation' (King James version), 'son of exhortation' or 'son of encouragement' (Revised standard version, Jerusalem Bible New International version). In Acts 13:1, prophet and teacher describe him and a list of other Christian leaders. In Lystra (Acts 14:12) Barnabas is even called 'Zeus' by pagan worshipers. In Acts 14:14 he is listed with Paul as an Apostle.

After the death of Stephen, many of the Hellenists filed North (Acts 8:1) but Barnabas stayed behind in Jerusalem with the Apostles. Barnabas also had family connections in Jerusalem; his cousin was named John Mark, whose mother Mary lived in Jerusalem and hosted the Church in her home (Acts 12:12). This same John Mark was to have a decisive role in the friendship of Barnabas and Paul.

Barnabas and Paul

Paul and Barnabas met a little while after Paul's Damascus road experience. After Paul had spent some time in Arabia, he returned to Jerusalem, but the Apostles were nervous of the new convert. They were more than justified in this, as Paul would admit later:

"You have surely heard how I have lived in the past, within Judaism, and how there was simply no limit to the ways I persecuted the church of God in my attempts to destroy it." (Gal 1:13)

And we find in the book of the *Acts* that Saul 'approved of thee the killing'—i.e. the martyrdom of Stephen (8:1).

"Barnabas, however, took charge of him, introduced him to the Apostles and explained how the Lord had appeared to him on his journey and how he had preached fearlessly at Damascus in the name of Jesus."
(Acts 9:27)

Barnabas here shows his flair for encouragement and his sense of the needs of the underdog. Paul did not feel he was an underdog. Barnabas had a deep appreciation of the real situation, and put himself out to smooth the path of the new convert.

Since the death of Stephen, the Church in Jerusalem had to live with a lot of fear. They felt the harshness of rejection by their fellow Jews, and were found to be more than a little confused. Now one of their persecutors wanted to become one of them. Where would this lead? Many would also struggle with the Lord's command to forgive enemies; old wounds could run deep.

To face these fears, Barnabas put himself out on a limb and eased Paul into the company of the Apostles. One would think that this was something Paul could never forget, but time was to prove the opposite. Paul certainly did get everything right first time round: but more later.

Missionary Travels

After a while getting to know the Apostles, Paul set sail from Cæsarea to Tarsus (Gal 1:18) while Barnabas remained in Jerusalem. However, the Church was growing in the Syrian city of Antic, and Barnabas was dispatched there (Acts 11:22). Under his guidance the Church grew even more, with Barnabas referred to as a 'good man, full of the Holy Spirit and faith' (Acts 11:24). Barnabas made contact with Paul and invited him to join the work in Antic. Together, Paul and Barnabas co-led the Church there for one year (Acts 11:26).

Things are harmonious thus far; the two got on well. Barnabas is prepared to celebrate his popularity and success with the new convert Paul. Barnabas is generous and protective, and there arose a genuine friendship between himself and Paul. Barnabas and Paul were responsible for giving to others by bringing relief to the Church in Jerusalem, threatened with famine. (Acts 11:30)

Meanwhile:

"In the church at Antic the following were called prophets and teachers: Barnabas, Simeon called Niger, and Lucius of Cyrene, Manaen, who had been brought up with Herod the Tetrach and Saul. One day while they were offering worship to the Lord and Keeping a fast the Holy Spirit said, I want Barnabas and Saul set apart for the work to which I have called them, so it was that after fasting and prayer they laid their hands on them and set them off." (Acts 13:1-3)

They decided to accept their role as missionaries and set sail for Cyprus. This decision might have been influenced by Barnabas who was from Cyprus (4:36). John Mark acted as their secretary (13:5) but when Barnabas and Paul, after their arrival in Pamplylia, decided to climb the mountain towards Antic,

John Mark turned back (Acts 13:13), This is passed over gently in Chapter 13, but Paul was harsh in his judgement of Mark: 'the man who deserted them' (Acts 15:38). Barnabas was more willing to forgive, and give the young man a chance to redeem himself. Storm clouds were beginning to gather.

There is another indication by Luke to put, in a very gentle way, that things were not all they should be. In Acts 13:2–7 Barnabas is listed first but, with Paul's confrontation with Elymas the magician at Paoles in Crete, it is always Paul who is main spokesman. This is seen again in Acts 13:44–45, where Paul now appears in charge. Barnabas is humble enough to allow Paul to come forward and be the chief spokesman; it must have cost him at another level. He had done so much, and given so much of himself. He was like a teacher, looking on a gifted student, achieving more than he ever did. It takes a lot of love and selflessness to allow this to happen, but it also leaves one feeling exposed and vulnerable. There is no doubt as regards Barnabas's love for Paul. Paul does not appear to have been so sensitive to this.

Break Point

In the new Church, the tensions experienced by Barnabas and Paul were reflected in different ways. As the Church sought out its identity in the world, the old Jewish world tried to establish itself in the new Church; there was an upsurge in Pharisaic observances, e.g. circumcision, and this tension was beginning to be felt especially in the new Church, which was now no longer exclusively Jewish. If these Judaism sects won out, Christianity would just become another Jewish sect. Some Jews came down to Antioch where Paul and Barnabas were. They tried to persuade the converts that they would lose everything unless they accepted Judaism. Paul and Barnabas argued strongly against this, and matters were at a deadlock. They appealed to Jerusalem for a ruling. It was clear that certain Pharisees had been converted, but tried to hold on to the law, especially circumcision.

It might be easy to judge these Judaists that were indeed against them. (e.g. Gal 3:6–18, 4:21–31, passim) It comes a lot closer to home when we see what they tried to do. They were devoted to the law (the Torah) and now they had to change their world view completely, and replace old ways of thinking with new. Their world was no more, and it was only rational to try and hanker after the values and things they left behind. There are echoes of this attitude in people who can't adapt to modern expressions of religion, and look back to the way things were. 'Wasn't it so much better then?' It is easy to be upset and feel there is nothing permanent, nothing to cling to, nothing to give shelter in the storm.

At the council Peter spoke (Acts 15:6–12). Peter led the council to ponder whether one could earn the favour of God? Or must one accept his own helplessness, and be ready in faith to accept what the grace of God brings; we could never put God in our debt. After Peter came James; they heard of the Jerusalem Church (Acts 15:13–21). He decreed that all disciples should be allowed into the Church without let or hindrance, and recommended a number of minor things for the Gentiles to observe so as not to scandalise their Jewish counterparts. This was then sent out by decree to the churches (Acts 15:21–37) and an uneasy peace reigned.

The next incident is not related by Luke in *Acts*, but it shows the strain the whole affair had caused, and in a particular way led to bad blood between Paul and Barnabas. Paul tells us that Peter came to Antioch and used to eat with the pagans, 'but after certain friends arrived he stopped doing this and kept away from them altogether for the group had insisted on circumcision.' The other Jews joined them in this pretence and even Barnabas felt himself obliged to deny their behaviour:

"When I saw they were not reflecting the true meaning of the Good News, I said to Cephas in front of everyone, 'in spite of being a Jew, you live like pagans and not like the Jews, so you have no right to make the pagans apply Jewish ways'." (Gal 1:14–15)

For Paul this matter was crucial, but being so completely right did bring casualties. John Moriarty, a hermit in the West of Ireland, speaks of being 'able to kill someone with the truth'. Paul was right, but did not take any prisoners among those who did not see things clearly. He did not spare Barnabas and Peter when they erred. Berating and humiliating Peter publicly, and not sparing Barnabas in his letter to the Galatians, Paul does not in any way come across as someone who could or would forgive weakness—at least, not yet! He still had to grow.

Storm Clouds

Paul was full of zeal and was all ready to go again. Barnabas was still with him, but by now well and truly playing second violin. Paul begins the dialogue with Barnabas:

"Let us go back and visit all the towns where we preached the word of the Lord, so that we can see how the others are doing." (Acts 15:36–38)

Barnabas suggested taking John Mark, but Paul was not enthusiastic about taking along the man who deserted them in Pamphylia and had refused to share in their work.

After a violent quarrel they parted company and Barnabas sailed off with Mark to Cyprus (Acts 15:36–39). The end came swiftly, too swiftly for all they had been through; it came also in the worst way possible for two great friends in the spirit. Violent words leave their mark on a person, and when all that remains are harsh words, then the ending is doubly sorrowful. We are not told any more that Paul and Barnabas made up; again; Luke passes serenely over this point. In 1 Cor 9:6 Paul mentions Barnabas, but it is not clear from this that they were ever reunited. Later on, in the same letter, Paul speaks in the following way:

"Love is always patient and kind, it is never jealous; love

is never boastful or conceited; it does not take offence and is not resentful. Love takes no pleasure in other people's sins but delights in the truth; it is always ready to excuse, to trust, to hope and to endure whatever comes." (1 Cor 13:4–8)

This was certainly not the way Paul treated Barnabas, but life and its hurts can become teachers too, messengers of the spirit. Paul must have been in some way self-aware and seen how he had hurt other people, good people. In his exhortation to the Corinthians, he pointed out a different ideal of love that others had found from him. The final argument had been over John, called Mark, and Paul was unwilling to forgive him and give him another chance.

How did Barnabas feel in this? It was, after all, he who had taken Paul under his wing when Paul himself needed forgiveness from a fearful Church (Acts 9:27). Barnabas had often stood up for Paul and, because of the respect and high regard Barnabas was held in, Paul was accepted. Now John Mark stood in need, and Paul slammed the door shut. Enough was enough, and their friendship was shortened with harsh words. Perhaps this was a disgrace for Paul; he had spurned a very good man and seen him leave. It is a hard part of life to realise that one can let others down. One of the stronger indicators for me, that Paul deepened in his conversion, is to be found in the *Second Letter to the Corinthians*.

"In view of the extraordinary nature of these revelations, to stop me from getting too proud I was given a thorn in the flesh, an angel of Satan to beat me and stop me from getting too proud. About this thing I have pleaded with the Lord three times for it to leave me, but he said, 'My grace is enough for thee.' My prayer is at its best in weakness, so I am happy to make weaknesses my special boast so that the power of Christ may stay over me, and that is why I am quite content with my weaknesses, and with insults, hardships, persecutions and the agonies I go through for Christ's sake. For it is when I am weak that I am strong." (2 Cor 12:7–10)

This is a different Paul from the 'untouchable' Paul who took the 'moral high ground'. This is an important addendum to the story. In the letter to Philemon we have an important mention:

"Epraphas, a prisoner with me in Christ Jesus, sends his greetings, so do my colleagues, Mark, Aristarbos, Demas and Luke." (Phil 24)

And we find:

"Get Mark to come and bring him with you. I find him a useful helper in my work." (2 Tim 4:11)

So in the end Paul did give Mark a second chance, as Barnabas had wished him to. A bit of Barnabas did rub off on Paul, and perhaps Paul's welcome of Mark was his way of showing how much he valued Barnabas after all.

A Story of Darkness

The story of Barnabas, John Mark and Paul was something of an eye-opener to me. It is a story involving personality clashes, breakdown in relationships and hurtful words. For me, John Mark is the same Mark who wrote the Gospel. There are many modern authors (e.g. Harrington etc.) who disagree with this position, but as yet no new identity for Mark has been found. The themes of reconciliation, making mistakes, and starting all over again, are found strongly in *The Gospel of Mark* (cf the figure Peter).

Mark only arrived at the state where he could write and appreciate these things by working through them himself. It took work by Paul to leave behind his position and go and meet Mark again. This meditation gives me food for thought. In the field of relationships, so much can get in the way, and a deep feeling of hurt can be left behind. In some way this can degenerate into harshness and bitterness, but if we can avoid this extreme then, like Paul and Mark, we can continue to work on our difficulties, and perhaps allow healing to come again.

Chapter Five

Mark and the Jesus of Self-Giving

W E have met Mark in Chapter Four where he became a
companion to Paul in the last days (Philemon 24, Col
4:10, 2 Tim 4:11). He had been an outcast and
something of an outlaw in the eyes of Paul (Acts 15:37ff).
Towards the end of Peter's life we find mention of Mark who
was among his trusted few (1 Peter 5:12–13). Mark then comes
from being an outcast to being one of the faithful disciples.
People wanted a record from these sources and Mark duly
obliged with the first Gospel.

In the last chapter, we looked at the importance of the
relationship between Jesus and the Father, and how this
relation-ship was seen in Jesus's life. How Jesus lived out his
life healing relationships, is mediated to us through the eyes of
Mark. We are called to enter into the same life-giving
relationship that Jesus had, but Mark had his own style of
showing us this.

Mark's Gospel is best described as 'passion-narrative' with a
long introduction. It is something of a dark gospel. I do not use
the word 'dark' in an evil sense, but more in the sense that the
Cross is presented in a stark, sombre fashion, and the Cross is
central because we see the Son of God humbled; yet this is
where He revealed Himself and allowed Himself to be seen.
Before we enter into a relationship with God in Jesus, then we
must see Him sad and crucified. This can seem like 'vanity' and
chasing the wind, but at the end of the narrative we come to
know ourselves better; in knowing God, we gain strength for
the journey, and as disciples we are able to take up our lives and
live them to the full. We have God with us. This takes us from
'chasing the wind' to embracing life. We are not spared hard
questions, wherever we are, whoever we are, but in God we find

a new impetus to live the questions, accept our crosses, and walk with Jesus.

The Passion Narrative

We begin our Marcan picture of Jesus just before the Garden of Gethsemene:

> "After the psalms had been sung they left for the Mount of Olives. And Jesus said to them, 'You will fall away, for the Scripture says: I shall strike the shepherd and the sheep will be scattered; however after my resurrection I shall go before you into Galilee. Peter said, 'Even if all fall away, I will not'" (Mk 14:28–29)

The disciples then looked at Jesus and did not understand. Then Jesus said again that he is destined to suffer. He tells them they will not survive the test. Peter chimes in that he will stand by Jesus. In an earlier moment Jesus had foretold the Passion. Peter tried to rebuke him but, turning and seeing his disciples, he rebuked Peter and said to him, 'Get behind me Satan!' (Mk 8:33) The thought of the Passion irritated the disciples. This was not the messiah of power they had hoped to see. This was not the man of power beside whom the sons of Zebedee had hoped to take places of pride. The disciples had formerly had struggles among themselves about who was actually the greatest. (9:33–37). Jesus was going to bring them face to face with the starkness of the Cross where all these questions would have to be re-evaluated.

> "They came to a plot of land called Gethsemene and he said to his disciples, 'Stay here while I pray.' Then he took Peter, James and John with him." (Mk 14:32–33)

Jesus had now entered His agony, and His moment of crisis had arrived. He could only face this moment with prayer that was His relationship with the Father. He was in anguish and He was in turmoil. He cried out:

"Abba, Father," he said, "for you everything is possible. Take this cup from me. But let it be as you, not I, would have it." (Mk 14:36)

Jesus is utterly crushed and is nervously exhausted. He asked Peter, James and John to stay with him, to be with him; but they slept, making his agony more profound still. He then turned to His Father and, using intimate terms, spoke, 'Abba, would that this might pass.' He shares His moment of doubt with the Father, telling Him that the spirit is indeed willing but the flesh is weak (14:38). Loneliness, depression, exhaustion are now the guests in the house of Jesus, and He feels He is going to be crushed by them. He chooses instead to trust in the will of His Father, the Abba, and He surrenders to His fate in this way.

'Abba' here denotes an intimate family relationship with the Father. It is wider than the translation 'Daddy' denotes. 'Abba' is a child's word for Father. It is also the intimate form of address between a son and his father, their 'I'—Thou'. It is the language of relationship. Jesus called us to have the same relationship with God, the Father. To say 'Abba' is to share a common relationship and a common inheritance with Jesus (Rom 8:16–17, Gal 4:6–7). The actual word 'Abba' does not occur anywhere else in the gospel apart from Mark 14:36 cited above but, in other parts of gospels where Jesus is seen in prayer, He uses the more formal Greek word 'Pater' which would translate the Aramaic 'Abba'.

He hoped, with all His might, that this lonely agony would not be His. He was in a high-anxiety state and this filled His every move. He had preferred that the disciples Peter, John and James would be with Him, but they slept. Jesus realises that the hour had come, He tells the disciples to sleep on and He abandoned Himself to His fate. Judas, one of the Twelve, betrays Him with a kiss and addresses Him as 'Rabbi'.

Before the crucifixion of Jesus, we see a young man follow Jesus dressed only in a linen cloth (14:51). He is caught hold of and runs away naked: a strong metaphor for the confusion of

Jesus's arrest. We pass over the scenes of the trial to the crowning with thorns:

"The soldiers led him away to the inner part of the Palace, that is called the Prætorium, and called the whole cohort together. They dressed him up in purple, twisted some thorns into a crown and put it on him." (15:16–18)

The soldiers were the first group of mockers; they had heard He was a king, and now they mocked the powerless one with shouts of, 'Hail king of the Jews.'

The disciples could see themselves in the ones that cried out for a show of power. The disciples ran as Jesus had warned them. Peter too, had denied Jesus. They were coming to see that the new kingdom would not be brought in by a powerful messiah. They were being asked to change and give themselves to God in a new way. Then Jesus is led away to be crucified. Mark's picture of the scene is frightening and raw:

"The passers by jeered at him, they shook their heads and said, 'Aha! So you would destroy the temple and rebuild it in three days. Then save yourself, come down from the cross.' The chief priests and the scribes mocked him among themselves in the same way; "He saved others, he cannot save himself.'" (15:29–31)

We have more and more mockers, all wondering what kind of man of power this was. They found it hard to believe that a messiah would suffer so, as the dregs of society would suffer. 'He saved others, let him save himself.' was the echo of the disciples' attitude during the gospel; they shunned the idea of Jesus. What we begin to see here is who would know Jesus. He died as an outcast and as an outsider. These were the ones who had understood Jesus. We can then look back in hindsight to such events, for example, in Jesus's Ministry, as the cure of the daughter of the Syro-Phœnician woman (7:24–30, 8:22–26), and the Gerasene demoniac (5:1–18), see also 5:21–43. Jesus leaves behind instructions to the demons and the outsiders who have been cured; he tells them not to tell others what they have recognised. All must come to their own realisation.

"When the sixth hour came there was darkness over the whole land until the ninth hour. And at the ninth hour Jesus cried out in a loud voice, 'Eloi, Eloi lama sabachtani?' which means, 'My God, my God, why have you forsaken me?'"

Jesus's agony comes across in an all-pervading sense of darkness. In agony, we have a reported speech of Jesus speaking in Aramaic, His mother's tongue. In agony people resort to their favourite prayers, in their native tongue. Jesus quotes Psalm 22.

This would indicate it was an important psalm for Jesus. In His dilemma, it was the one that said most to Him. Psalm 22 is a psalm which speaks of the sufferings and hopes of the just. The first verse goes as follows:

"My God, My God, why have you forsaken Me?
The words of my groaning do nothing to save me.
My God, I call by day but you do not answer, at night,
but I find no respite."

The psalm goes on to use images that express dehumanisation and the sense of being an outsider—shades of Job here. The just man is mocked and jeered. It is interesting to remember how Jesus was mocked, and how appropriate Psalm 22 is:

"But I am a worm, less than human,
Scorn of mankind, contempt of the people;
All who jeer at me,
They sneer and wag their heads,
He trusted himself to Yahweh, let Yahweh set him free!
Let him deliver him, as he took such a delight in him."

(v.6–8)

This psalm was written a long time before Jesus was born. It's frightening to see how accurately the Psalmist describes the agony of Jesus. He combines using images of savage dogs, fierce bulls to illustrate how the good are dehumanised.

The psalm changes to a psalm of thanksgiving. The psalm has carried the cries of the just, the innocent sufferer and called out to God. This motive we have already seen in Job, now in the psalms and in Jesus. The psalm exults that God hears the pain of the crushed. The situation is not altered, but now the downtrodden, the broken hearted have found a home in God:

"For he had not despised
nor disregarded the poverty of the poor,
has not turned away his face,
but has listened to the cry for help.
The poor will eat and be filled,
those who seek Yahweh will praise him.
May your heart live forever," (v.26)

Jesus is the living embodiment of the psalm. He shows us God hears our cry, our pain and we are now in an unbreakable bond of fellowship with Jesus, the suffering servant.

In the final verse of this psalm, all are called to come and remember Yahweh. Initially it is only an outsider; the broken-hearted also see that Yahweh is there in the middle of the storm of human degradation. This, in turn, calls others to join, and in their intercessions remember the sick and the deceased. (vs.27–31)

Psalm 22 belongs to a liturgical setting. This has important echoes for Mark. We see this in Mk 14:27–28. We note the setting is an Eucharistic meal. Jesus has presented the cup and the bread, telling the disciples, 'This is my Body, This is my Blood.' The disciples are caught in a bond of friendship with Jesus which will not be broken, even by their denial. We remember this in our celebration of the Eucharist; God does not withdraw His friendship, yet it is sadly in our power to betray God and His friendship. What therefore matters is that

God hears the cries of the just one (cf Ps 22) and we are called to reconciliation with God in Jesus, and from there live our lives of faith to the full.

In the *Gospel of Mark* we have two separate accounts of the feeding of the multitude (6:35–44 and 8:1–10). In Chapter 14 we have Jesus himself feeding the disciples in the form of Eucharistic bread. New life is offered to the disciples, who for a while sleep.

Now we come to the death of Jesus:

"But Jesus gave a cry and breathed his last. And the veil of the Sanctuary was torn in two from top to bottom. The centurion, who was standing in front of him, had seen how he died, and he said, 'In truth this man was the Son of God.'" (15:37–40)

Jesus's death is at once horrible and real. The 'veil of the Sanctuary' is a metaphor for such a tragic act calling out to heaven. The centurion is an important witness. He saw the way Jesus died and he was inspired to an act of faith, saying that this was truly the 'Son of God'. Once again, the outsider and outcasts are the ones with the clearest vision.

The story comes to an end in Chapter 16. The passage 16:1–8 is regarded by scholars as the end of the *Gospel of Mark*. The Chapter begins with Mary of Magdala, Mary, the mother of James, and Salome bringing spices to the tomb. Women, in Mark's Gospel, played an important part in the life of Jesus. They too––e.g. Mary of Magdala––could be said to be outsiders in a fiercely patriarchal society. They were the ones who stood by the Cross. These are the ones who see Jesus clearly. It is always the outsider, the unwanted one, who finds a friend in Christ.

They meet a young man at the tomb. One remembers back to the young man who typified the confusion when Jesus was arrested (14:51–52). Here we have a more tranquil scene. The stone has been rolled away, and when they entered they saw the young man and were filled with amazement:

"But he said to them, 'There is no need to be so amazed. You are looking for Jesus of Nazareth who was crucified; he has risen, he is not here. See, here is the place where they laid him. But you must go and tell his disciples and Peter, he is going ahead of you to Galilee; that is where you will see him, just as he told you." (16:6–7)

The women became apostles to the apostles. The apostles are at once offered reconciliation and new life. Jesus gave His life so that others would have life and live it to the full. This is what the centurion saw when he saw how Jesus died. He also gave his life for others so that they might live. This is what the outsider saw throughout the Gospel. Peter and the disciples could not see that the kingdom proclaimed by Jesus (10:23–25, 47:10–15 Passim) is not one of power but one of love, of self giving, of new life. The fellowship of the Eucharistic table is the same fellowship we carry through life. We are nourished by the Eucharistic body and blood of Jesus.

Mark, when he paints pictures of people, does not spare people's blushes. The disciples did not understand, and slept at times of trouble. They failed Jesus by denying Him. Yet Jesus never broke His bond of friendship, and always sent out a reconciling message to those who wronged Him. The outcasts and the outsiders always found in Jesus a brother who cared and His love made a difference in their lives.

The message at the end of Mark is very painful. Mark shows us the power of reconciliation and forgiveness—his own life—and that those who feel they do not belong, who feel they are outsiders, do find a love and a friend in Jesus. It is not just a statement that the broken-hearted belong. It is an invitation to receive the new life Jesus offered us. He died so that we might have life, and face life's question with His heart.

The Cross of Love

In *Mark* we see a very human Christ, who was in mental agony, who was abandoned yet his love comes through. At the meal with the disciples, there was a bond of love and fellowship which Jesus would maintain; that is why He told Peter and others to wait for Him in Galilee.

In the garden scene, mental agony cannot drive Him away from offering His love, and finally, in His hour of agony, He does not withdraw His promise. That causes the centurion to cry out that this was in truth the Son of God (14:30). The centurion stands for those who feel deserted, isolated or hurt by life and people. Now all these people have found a brother whose love is stronger than death, and whose life and love we are invited to share. We do belong, and Jesus has gone before us to show us we are cherished by God.

Mark, with all his unique style of writing, was in a very strong position to appreciate how deeply this forgiving love can mean to a person (cf his portrayal of Peter) and the healing power of forgiving love is visible in Mark's Passion account.

A new hope dawns with the love of Jesus Christ.

Epilogue

Philemon

TO try and catch the wind, to try and find answers to the innumerable questions that life poses, is daunting. When life's sadness comes to one's house in whatever form, then the world changes for one for ever. Betrayal of trust by a loved one—abuse, whether sexual, physical, psychological or verbal—can leave a person shattered, broken, and often times good people fall into despair and, tragically, suicide.

We have looked at people whose lives were broken for different reasons. I have not looked at the issues that brought people to their destiny. What I have looked at is how life and its sadness can change people. To come to terms with life, and re-form a relationship with God and the world is like trying to 'catch the wind'. Indeed, when the going is really rough, it can be like chasing the wind and 'vanity'. The human spirit, however, is indomitable, and this is the place where we meet God and grow into a new person.

Paul's letter to Philemon illustrates what I am trying to say. Onesimus is a runaway slave who has come to look after Paul. We do not have runaway slaves, but we do have our own issues that hurt us and make life difficult. For Philemon and his household, their trouble came in the form of a runaway slave, who perhaps had stolen property as well:

"But if he has wronged you in any way or owes you anything, then let me pay for it." (Phil 18)

By their first assent of faith, Philemon and his household have embraced a new way of life in this world. Onesimus was a slave, and in the old world was a person of no rights; and in society the 'owner' of a slave was bound to uphold the way of

83

life of his time. Enter Onesimus. He was a slave, a runaway slave at that, property of Philemon, but now equal in dignity to his 'owner' and 'master'. This is how Philemon's faith came to be questioned. We are not given a solution by Paul because, when faced with life's hard questions, one can feel lost and solutions don't come easily (Job). However, our faith and life become healed as we face the questions. We go from life's hard questions—which can seem impossible from a God we no longer know—and perhaps have come to doubt. Yet this is a story of trying to catch the wind, and our wounds can become sources of healing for others as well as ourselves. We go from life to God and His word, and from His word to life.

I leave you with a fantasy exercise. Put yourself in the place of Philemon, a rich man who owned slaves. Onesimus ran away, was a Christian; now he was coming back. How would you receive him? What punishment—if any—would you give? What would all your friends think if you welcomed a slave back without punishment; not alone without punishment, but as a member of your household? Your high rank in society is threatened by someone who has hurt you, and you are going to lose your place in society in welcoming back the person who has landed you in this mess. Philemon's problems are not mine or yours, but his problem can throw into sharp relief our own. You have in the end to find your own way to God, and your solution to His problems. However, as Paul cleverly points out in his letter to Philemon, the journey is no longer a lonely one. He says at the end of the letter, 'May the grace of Our Lord Jesus Christ be with your Spirit' (Phil 25). We have our own issues, and we have the example of good people who have gone before us. Solutions are not instant but, with the power of God's love, we can embrace the questions and work towards living life to the full.

Now put yourself in the place of Philemon and listen to the Letter from Paul to Philemon:

"... I always mention you in my prayers and thank God for you, because I hear of the love and faith which you have for the Lord Jesus and for all the saints. I pray that this faith will give rise to a sense of fellowship that will show you all the good things that we are able to do for Christ. I am so delighted and comforted, to know of your love; they tell me, brother, how you have put a new heart into the saints. Now, although in Christ I can have no diffidence about telling you to do whatever is duty, I am appealing to your love instead, reminding you that this is Paul writing, an old man now and, what is more, still a prisoner of Jesus Christ.

"I am appealing to you for a child of mine, whose father I became while wearing these chains: I mean Onesimus. He was no use to you before, but will be useful to you now, as he has been to me. I am sending him back to you, and with him—I could say—a part of my own self. I should have liked to keep him with me; he could have been a substitute for you, to help me while I am in the chains that the good news has brought me. However, I do not want to do anything without your consent; it would have been forcing your act of kindness, which should be spontaneous. I know you have been deprived of Onesimus for a time, but it was only so that you could have him back forever, not as a slave any more, but something much better than a slave, a dear brother; especially dear to me, but how much more to you, as a blood-brother as well as a brother in the Lord. So if all that we have in common means anything to you, welcome him as you would me; but if he has wronged you in any way or owes you anything, then let me pay for it. I am writing this in my own handwriting: I Paul, shall pay it back—I will not add any mention of your own debt to me, which is yourself. Well then, brother, I am counting on you, in the Lord; put new heart into me in Christ. I am writing with complete confidence in your compliance, sure that you will do even more than I ask.

"There is another thing: will you get a place ready for me to stay in? I am hoping through my prayers to be restored to you.

"Epaphas, a prisoner with me in Jesus Christ, sends his greetings; so do my colleagues, Mark, Aristarchus, Demas and Luke.

"May the grace of our Lord Jesus Christ be with your spirit."

GLOSSARY OF BIBLICAL TERMS

Acts of the Apostles

This is the fifth book of the New Testament in the common arrangement. It records certain phases of the progress of Christianity for a period of thirty years after Jesus's death and resurrection. *Acts* was originally written as a sequel to the *Gospel of Luke*, by the same author.

Aramaic

This is a Semitic language related to Hebrew. From the Sixth Century B.C.E. Aramaic continued to spread in the vernacular in the Palestinian region and was in general use in Palestine in the First Century B.C.E. It was the language spoken by Jesus. What we have in the New Testament was written in Greek, but fragments of what Jesus originally said are still to be found – e.g. 'Abba' as an address for 'Father' in Aramaic, recorded in the Greek Gospels.

Behemoth

A mythical beast, described in Job 40:15—24, as the first of God's creation. It is frequently associated with the hippopotamus – as Levantian associated with the crocodile. However, not all the descriptions of the creature describe the hippopotamus. He was seen as a symbol of cosmic evil.

Canon

This is a Greek word which signifies a rule, noun or measure. With the Bible it identifies these writings which different religious communities – Jews, Protestants, Catholic, Orthodox – considered to be normative for their faiths.

Covenant

In general this is a contract or agreement entered into by two parties with a view to the mutual advantage of each. In the Bible it is a bond or 'testament' between God and a person (Noah – Gen 9:18—17, Abraham – Gen 17:1—8), or a group of people (Ex 24:4—8). Christians speak of the 'New Testament' that God has entered into with all humankind in Christ.

Diaspora

Diaspora is a Greek word meaning dispersion. It was formed as a result of the deportation of the population of Judah by the Babylonians in 579 and 587—586 B.C.E. that resulted in the formation of a new permanent community outside of Judah. After the Babylonian Empire fell, the Persian King Cyrus allowed the exiles to return home. Some remained, and a commonwealth of exiles was established, i.e. the Diaspora. Paul belonged to the Diaspora.

Didache

The 'Didache' or the 'Teaching of the Twelve Apostles' is a late First Century or very early Second Century manual of moral and liturgical instructions used in the catechises of the early Church, especially the Gentile Christians.

Exile

This refers to the fall of Judah and Israel and the subsequent deportation of their peoples. In the ancient East, deportation was used against conquered peoples (Am 1). From 734 B.C.E. the entire kingdom underwent this. The greatest deportations, that left a mark on the people of the covenant, were those resulting from the campaign of Nebuchadnezzar against Judah and Jerusalem in 597, 587, 528, (2 Ecs 24:14, 25:11, Jr 52:28 ff). It is these deportations into Babylon for which the name of 'Exile' has been reserved. Eventually Babylon fell and King Cyrus, in

538 B.C.E., allowed the people to return. This led to the time of the post-exile – or post-exilic times, where the people had to come to terms with their shattered world.

Frankincense

Frankincense is an aromatic gum-resin that emits a strong pleasant odour when burned.

Hebrew

This is the language in which the Old Testament was written. Hebrew, too, is a name occasionally applied to the early Israelites. In the New Testament the term designates Jews. In modern usage, the term 'Hebrew' is generally applied to the language of ancient and modern Israel, and of Jewish scripture and traditions .

Israel

The name Israel – be consecrated by God – is confirmed on Jacob by a divine messenger after their struggle at the Waddi Jabbok (Gen 32:28, 35:10, Hos 12:3). The twelve sons of Jacob and their tribal descendants are therefore called the 'sons of Israel'.

Israel remained the designation for the entire nation until the division of the kingdom in 924 B.C.E. (Kings 12:1—20). Biblical authors term the ten Northern tribes, i.e. the Northern Kingdom, Israel, and the two Southern tribes, i.e. the Southern Kingdom, Judah. Hence, after the Northern Kingdom falls, in 722 B.C.E., and only Jerusalem remains, its residents are called 'Judalites' or 'Judeans'. In the post-exilic period the residents of Judah are regularly called 'Jews', but the term 'Israel' is also used.

Kingdom of God

The term designates not a political or geographical entity, but the reign, or rule, of God reprehensibly present in our midst through the power of the Holy Spirit. Inaugurated by Jesus, and central to the mission of the Church, it is the goal – already starting to be realised – that God wills for the whole of creation.

Levianthan

This is a mythological sea master who is one of the primeval adversaries of the storm God. In Job 41, Levianthan is described as a pet under God's control. Many commentators of Job have seen, in the description of Levianthan, something similar to the description of a crocodile. In late literature, Thomas Hobbes (1651 C.E.) gives the title *Levianthan* to his work, and Levianthan is the symbolic name for the absolute power of the commonwealth.

Myrrh

An aromatic gum resin found in Arabia and Eastern Africa. According to the Bible, Myrrh was traded from Canaan to Egypt (Gen 37:25, 43:11). 'Liquid Myrrh' (Myrrh-scented oil) was a cosmetic (Esther 2:122, Song of Songs 5:5). In the New Testament it was used as a painkiller (mixed with wine, Mk 15:23) and to anoint corpses after death.

Passover

This festival, observed on the fourteenth day of the month of Nasion (March—April) commemorates the exodus of the Hebrews from Egypt.

Post Exilic

This refers to the term of restoration, when the Jews were about to return home to their own land and set about rebuilding the Temple.

Sheol

In Hebrew thought this was where the dead are thought to exist in darkness, dust and helplessness (Job 17:13—16, Ps 88:3—12, Is 14:9—11). In later development of thought came the resurrection of the dead (Wis 2:13—3:1, Dn 2:12, Mtt 28:18, Mk 16, Ac 23:6, Rom 1:4, 1 Cor 15, Pl 2:9—11, Heb 2:10).

Wasf

This is the praise of each other's bodily features found in the *Song of Songs*. Traditionally, in the love poetry of the ancient Far East, it was the poetry within the bridegroom for the bride, and by the bride for the bridegroom. In the poetry they praised each other for their physical charms.

Yahweh

This is the proper name for God in the Hebrew Bible. The Hebrew word-name denotes 'majesty' and we find the translation 'Lord' (Is 1:24, 3:1). It is the name revealed to Moses, and treasured as a sign of intimacy and favour. (Ex 3:13, 34:6).

ABBREVIATIONS

Old Testament

Genesis	Gn	Proverbs	Prv
Exodus	Ex	Qoheleth	Qo
Leviticus	Lv	Song of Songs	Sg
Numbers	Nm	Wisdom	Wis
Deuteronomy	Dt	Sirach	Sir
Joshua	Jos	Isaiah	Is
Judges	Jgs	Jeremiah	Jer
Ruth	Ru	Lamentations	Lam
1 Samuel	1 Sm	Baruch	Bar
2 Samuel	2 Sm	Ezekiel	Ez
1 Kings	1 Kgs	Daniel	Dn
2 Kings	2 Kgs	Hosea	Hos
1 Chronicles	1 Chr	Joel	Jl
2 Chronicles	2 Chr	Amos	Am
Ezra	Ezr	Obadiah	Ob
Nehemiah	Neh	Jonah	Jon
Tobit	Tb	Micah	Mi
Judith	Jdt	Nahum	Na
Esther	Est	Habakkuk	Hb
1 Maccabees	1 Mc	Zephaniah	Zep
2 Maccabees	2 Mc	Haggai	Hg
Job	Jb	Zechariah	Zec
Psalms	Ps(s)	Malachi	Mal

New Testament

Matthew	Mt		1 Corinthians	1 Cor
Mark	Mk		2 Corinthians	2 Cor
Luke	Lk		Galatians	Gal
John	Jn		Ephesians	Eph
Acts of the Apostles	Acts	Philippians	Phil

New Testament Continued

Romans	Rom	Colossians	Col
1 Thessalonians	1 Thes	1 Peter	1 Pt
2 Thessalonians	2 Thes	2 Peter	2 Pt
1 Timothy	1 Tm	1 John	1 Jn
2 Timothy	2 Tm	2 John	2 Jn
Titus	Ti	3 John	3Jn
Philemon	Phlm	Jude	Jude
Hebrews	Heb	Revelation	Rv
James	Jas		

General

B.C.E.	Before Common Era (instead of B.C.)
C.E.	Common Era (instead of A.D.)